# Credits

**Author**
Craig Gilchrist

**Reviewers**
Ankush Agrawal
Long Tran
Tian Zhang

**Commissioning Editor**
Kunal Parikh

**Acquisition Editor**
Reshma Raman

**Content Development Editor**
Manasi Pandire

**Technical Editor**
Mrunmayee Patil

**Copy Editors**
Janbal Dharmaraj
Sayanee Mukherjee

**Project Coordinator**
Leena Purkait

**Proofreaders**
Simran Bhogal
Maria Gould
Ameesha Green
Paul Hindle

**Indexer**
Monica Ajmera Mehta

**Graphics**
Abhinash Sahu

**Production Coordinator**
Nilesh R. Mohite

**Cover Work**
Nilesh R. Mohite

# About the Author

**Craig Gilchrist** is the Digital Director at Eden Agency (`http://createdineden.com/`), a small but mighty digital agency that is at the forefront of proximity marketing. His team is one of the first to release commercial iBeacon-powered apps in the world and currently boast over 1.5 million app downloads in multiple fields and have a perfectly balanced technical and creative team.

Craig is based in North Yorkshire, England, and has been developing commercial software since graduating from the University of Teesside in 2004 with a BSc in Software Engineering and has been building apps for iOS since 2009.

Craig is an avid reader and is always at the forefront of commercial technological developments. Other than mobile app development and digital marketing, Craig also has a keen interest in developing rich media, including gaming, children's interactive media, and a very keen interest in Unity and virtual reality with Oculus Rift.

> First, I'd like to thank my baby boy, Teddy, for being my raison d'être. I know you don't know it yet, but I never knew what life meant before you arrived. As you grow and blossom, I hope I'm as inspiring to you as you are to me, I'm already so proud of you son.
>
> I would also like to thank my wife, Ria, for being a beacon of support throughout the writing of this book. Your new mummy voice is the stern voice I need to kick me into shape. You're beautiful, patient, and majestic. You're my fairy tale and my happily ever after.
>
> Finally, I'd like to thank my team at Eden Agency (`@createdineden`) who I'm proud to call my friends, for being so creative, innovative, and generally awesome, and for keeping me on my toes. May we continue to build exquisite solutions for long.

# Learning iBeacon

Build proximity applications for iOS using Apple's groundbreaking iBeacon technology

**Craig Gilchrist**

BIRMINGHAM - MUMBAI

# Learning iBeacon

Copyright © 2014 Packt Publishing

All rights reserved. No part of this book may be reproduced, stored in a retrieval system, or transmitted in any form or by any means, without the prior written permission of the publisher, except in the case of brief quotations embedded in critical articles or reviews.

Every effort has been made in the preparation of this book to ensure the accuracy of the information presented. However, the information contained in this book is sold without warranty, either express or implied. Neither the author, nor Packt Publishing, and its dealers and distributors will be held liable for any damages caused or alleged to be caused directly or indirectly by this book.

Packt Publishing has endeavored to provide trademark information about all of the companies and products mentioned in this book by the appropriate use of capitals. However, Packt Publishing cannot guarantee the accuracy of this information.

First published: November 2014

Production reference: 1181114

Published by Packt Publishing Ltd.
Livery Place
35 Livery Street
Birmingham B3 2PB, UK.

ISBN 978-1-78439-712-8

www.packtpub.com

# About the Reviewers

**Ankush Agrawal** is a third year undergraduate student studying Computer Science and Business at the University of California, San Diego. He is a self-taught iOS developer who also has a passion for Bluetooth low energy. He has utilized BLE in various forms for award-winning hackathon projects and is eagerly working to discover its full potential. He has interned at The Boeing Company for the past two summers and is now seeking opportunities in Silicon Valley.

**Long Tran** is a student at the University of California, San Diego (class of 2016), where he studies Computer Science and Business. He loves challenging himself outside school by interning at Fortune 500 companies and exploring new technology trends. He has put iBeacon to good uses in his most recent iOS side projects. After graduation, Long plans to work at an established company with a start-up culture, where he hopes to learn a thing or two to start his own business.

**Tian Zhang** is a freelancer working in the field of iOS development, Bluetooth low energy, and home automation.

# www.PacktPub.com

## Support files, eBooks, discount offers, and more

For support files and downloads related to your book, please visit www.PacktPub.com.

Did you know that Packt offers eBook versions of every book published, with PDF and ePub files available? You can upgrade to the eBook version at www.PacktPub.com and as a print book customer, you are entitled to a discount on the eBook copy. Get in touch with us at service@packtpub.com for more details.

At www.PacktPub.com, you can also read a collection of free technical articles, sign up for a range of free newsletters and receive exclusive discounts and offers on Packt books and eBooks.

https://www.packtpub.com/books/subscription/packtlib

Do you need instant solutions to your IT questions? PacktLib is Packt's online digital book library. Here, you can search, access, and read Packt's entire library of books.

## Why subscribe?

- Fully searchable across every book published by Packt
- Copy and paste, print, and bookmark content
- On demand and accessible via a web browser

## Free access for Packt account holders

If you have an account with Packt at www.PacktPub.com, you can use this to access PacktLib today and view 9 entirely free books. Simply use your login credentials for immediate access.

# Table of Contents

**Preface**     **1**

**Chapter 1: Welcome to iBeacon**     **7**
  **Introducing iBeacon**     7
  **Hey, 'sup**     8
  **Understanding a range using RSSI**     9
  **Compatible devices**     10
  **Commercial applications of iBeacon**     11
  **So many vendors, so little time**     12
    Estimote     13
      Estimote beacons – pros     15
      Estimote beacons – cons     15
    ROXIMITY     15
      ROXIMITY beacons – pros     17
      ROXIMITY beacons – cons     17
    RedBearLab     18
      RedBear Beacon B1 – pros     19
      RedBear Beacon B1 – cons     20
    Other vendor options     20
  **The companion OS X application and website**     21
    Using the companion app     22
  **Hello world**     23
    Let's get started     24
    Adding the Core Location framework     25
    Adding a permission message     27
    Configuring the CLLocationManagerDelegate method     27
    Adding a CLLocationManager instance     28
    Preparing UUID     28
    Start monitoring     28
      Line by line     29

*Table of Contents*

| | |
|---|---|
| Testing our code | 30 |
| Summary | 32 |
| **Chapter 2: Detecting Beacons – Showing an Advert** | **33** |
| Uses of the UUID/major/minor broadcasting triplet | 33 |
| UUID – Universally Unique Identifier | 33 |
| Major | 35 |
| Minor | 35 |
| An example of a use case | 35 |
| Understanding Core Location | 36 |
| The CLBeaconRegion class | 36 |
| The CLLocationManager class | 37 |
| Creating a CLLocationManager class | 37 |
| Defining a CLLocationManager class line by line | 37 |
| locationManager:didEnterRegion | 38 |
| locationManager:didExitRegion | 39 |
| locationManager:didRangeBeacons:inRegion | 39 |
| locationManager:didChangeAuthorizationStatus | 40 |
| Understanding iBeacon permissions | 40 |
| Location permissions in iOS 8 | 41 |
| Enabling the location after denying it | 42 |
| Building the tutorial app | 43 |
| Creating the app | 43 |
| Adding CLOfferViewController | 43 |
| Setting location permission settings | 44 |
| Adding some controls | 44 |
| Setting up our root view controller | 45 |
| Configuring our location manager | 46 |
| Wiring up CLLocationManagerDelegate | 47 |
| Showing the advert | 49 |
| Dismissing the offer | 51 |
| Summary | 53 |
| **Chapter 3: Broadcasting Advertisements – Sending Offers** | **55** |
| Introducing the Core Bluetooth framework | 55 |
| Understanding centrals and peripherals | 55 |
| The Core Bluetooth framework, centrals, and peripherals | 56 |
| The CBCentral class | 56 |
| The CBPeripheral class | 57 |
| The CBPeripheralManager class | 57 |
| Obtaining broadcast values from CLBeaconRegion | 57 |
| Measured power (TXPower) | 58 |
| Let's get started | 58 |
| Adding frameworks | 59 |

[ ii ]

|  |  |
|---|---|
| Setting up our controls | 59 |
| Creating our views | 60 |
| Wiring up the storyboard | 61 |
| Setting up our view controller | 62 |
| Adding our switch logic | 63 |
| **Summary** | **65** |

## Chapter 4: Ranging Beacons – Hunting for Treasure    67

| | |
|---|---|
| **There be treasure nearby** | **67** |
| **Understanding distance** | **68** |
| **Our application** | **70** |
| **Getting started with building our app** | **71** |
| Drawing our initial views | 72 |
| Adding frameworks and project settings | 73 |
| Adding images | 73 |
| Building the root view controller | 74 |
| Building the treasure view controller | 75 |
| Finally, wire it up | 78 |
| Building the hunter view controller | 78 |
| Hunter view controller states | 79 |
| Imports and public properties | 80 |
| Private properties | 80 |
| Loading the view | 81 |
| Entering and exiting the region | 82 |
| Changing the state | 82 |
| Tidying up | 85 |
| Being extra conscientious | 85 |
| **Completing the code** | **85** |
| **Summary** | **86** |

## Chapter 5: Detecting Beacons in the Background – Location Dating    87

| | |
|---|---|
| **Real-life use cases** | **88** |
| An example use case for retail loyalty | 88 |
| An example use case for airline assistance | 88 |
| **Handing over responsibility** | **89** |
| **The CLBeaconRegion options** | **90** |
| **Passbook integration** | **91** |
| **Our tutorial app** | **93** |
| The scenario | 93 |
| Viewing anatomy | 94 |
| The code | 95 |
| Creating the application | 95 |
| Creating the view | 95 |

*Table of Contents*

| | |
|---|---|
| Configuring the app delegate | 96 |
| Implementing our view controller | 101 |
| **Testing your application** | **104** |
| Testing the beacons | 105 |
| Testing the passbook pass | 105 |
| **Summary** | **106** |
| **Chapter 6: Leaving Regions – Don't Forget Your Stuff** | **107** |
| **Raspberry Pi** | **108** |
| **Ninja Blocks** | **108** |
| **Nest** | **108** |
| **Phillips Hue** | **109** |
| **Belkin WeMo** | **109** |
| **iBeacon and home automation** | **109** |
| **Beacon stickers** | **110** |
| **Our tutorial** | **111** |
| Ranging beacons in the background | 111 |
| Tracking locations using background modes | 112 |
| Cheating the system | 113 |
| **Building our app** | **113** |
| Beginning the app with a database schema | 113 |
| Using a little helper | 114 |
| Master view controller implementation | 116 |
| Configuring the view controller | 117 |
| Fetching data from the Core Data framework | 118 |
| Configuring the table cell | 119 |
| Notifying the user | 120 |
| Inserting new objects | 121 |
| Ranging beacons | 121 |
| Detailed view controller implementation | 122 |
| Configuring the view | 123 |
| Getting and setting properties | 124 |
| Validating input | 125 |
| Finishing off UI | 125 |
| Adding NSLocationAlwaysUsageDescription | 126 |
| Enabling the background mode | 126 |
| **Testing your app** | **127** |
| **Summary** | **127** |
| **Chapter 7: Vendor SDKs – Buying and Configuring Beacons** | **129** |
| **Estimote motes and SDK** | **129** |
| **ROXIMITY implementation** | **130** |
| **Choosing the best platform for your requirements** | **130** |
| **AltBeacon – the open beacon specification** | **130** |

[ iv ]

*Table of Contents*

| | |
|---|---|
| **Using Estimote API 2.1** | **131** |
| Security | 131 |
| Estimote SDK classes | 132 |
| ESTBeacon | 132 |
| ESTBeaconDelegate | 132 |
| ESTBeaconManager | 133 |
| ESTBeaconManagerDelegate | 133 |
| **Let's get building** | **133** |
| Adding EstimoteSDK | 134 |
| Adding API access | 135 |
| The helper class | 135 |
| Configuring the master view controller | 136 |
| Configuring our beacon manager | 137 |
| Configuring the detail view controller | 138 |
| Configuring the view | 139 |
| Connecting and disconnecting from beacons | 140 |
| Saving the changes | 141 |
| Creating the view | 144 |
| **Testing your application** | **145** |
| **Summary** | **145** |
| **Chapter 8: Advanced Tutorial – iBeacon Museum** | **147** |
| **Our exhibitions** | **147** |
| **The museum map** | **149** |
| **Our app structure** | **149** |
| The permission view | 149 |
| The atrium view | 150 |
| The exhibit view | 150 |
| **The supporting website** | **150** |
| Tracking our user's journey | 151 |
| **Our app design** | **152** |
| **Building the application** | **153** |
| Creating the project | 153 |
| Initializing the views | 153 |
| Adding the CoreLocation functionality | 155 |
| Determining the first view | 155 |
| Configuring our permission view | 157 |
| Adding controls | 158 |
| Configuring the exhibit view | 160 |
| Adding controls to the exhibit view | 161 |
| Adding content methods | 162 |
| Ranging beacons | 163 |
| Configuring our atrium view | 165 |
| Adding atrium view controls | 165 |

[ v ]

| | |
|---|---|
| **Time to test** | **167** |
| **Summary** | **167** |
| **Chapter 9: iBeacon Security – Understanding the Risks** | **169** |
| **Beacon spoofing** | **169** |
| Defending against beacon spoofing | 170 |
| Rotating UUIDs | 171 |
| **Beacon hacking** | **171** |
| **Dispelling security myths** | **172** |
| **Overcoming users' fears with good UX** | **172** |
| **Summary** | **173** |
| **Index** | **175** |

# Preface

The iBeacon technology is the most disruptive technology in the field of interaction design. Formally, iBeacon is simply a protocol defined by Apple and built on top of Bluetooth 4.0. Creatively, iBeacon is your passport to apps that truly interact with the world around them.

Imagine your shopping list becoming an interactive map of the supermarket, your phone turning the porch lights on as you drive down the street, or ordering your meal at your favorite table in your favorite restaurant without ever speaking with a waiter. All this and more is made possible with iBeacon.

Taking a practical and pragmatic approach, this book will introduce you to the concepts and applications of iBeacon technology for providing proximity-based solutions to iOS devices. We cover everything from prototyping simple scenarios to building a fully-functional interactive museum app, all using Xcode and Apple's Core Location and Core Bluetooth frameworks.

This book is designed to cover easy-to-follow examples to introduce the core features of iBeacon technology solutions, from discovering beacons and using your iOS device as a beacon, to some more powerful tutorials that closely match real-world examples.

Everything in this book can be applied to your own developments, but is done in a way which breaks down each element of the technology and the supporting iOS SDKs. Soon, you will be armed with all the tools and to produce interactive proximity-powered solutions with ease.

Finally, this book comes with an OS X app that lets you use your Mac as an iBeacon so that you can get to grips with the technology without having to buy any beacons.

# What this book covers

*Chapter 1, Welcome to iBeacon*, introduces you to the technology and the incredible opportunities it offers us as developers. We'll cover the technological advancements that have made iBeacon possible and we'll discuss some of the options which you have to get your hands on for some real beacons. Finally, we'll create the age-old Hello World application and start detecting beacons easily.

*Chapter 2, Detecting Beacons – Showing an Advert*, introduces you to beacon detection in more detail. We'll show you how to differentiate between beacons using the values that they broadcast and we'll introduce the concept of regions and some of the CoreLocation classes used to represent regions and location. We will also cover the user permissions needed to monitor beacons before building a tutorial using our new-found knowledge to build an app that shows different offers as you approach different beacons.

*Chapter 3, Broadcasting Advertisements – Sending Offers*, introduces you to the important classes in the Core Bluetooth framework and discusses how to handle the variations in beacon broadcasting power before building a functioning beacon broadcasting app. Now that you know how to detect beacons and act on their unique broadcasting values, you will learn how to turn your iPhone or iPad into a fully functioning iBeacon broadcaster.

*Chapter 4, Ranging Beacons – Hunting for Treasure*, introduces the concept of ranging beacons and determining their distance from the receiver. This chapter expands on the CLLocationManager class usage and will take you through a tutorial that allows one device to be configured as a sender and another as a receiver to ultimately build a simple treasure-hunting app.

*Chapter 5, Detecting Beacons in the Background – Location Dating*, introduces you to the core responsibilities of the iOS in monitoring beacons in the background. We will discuss how iOS takes over beacon monitoring when the app is in the background and will also launch the app if it has been terminated.

*Chapter 6, Leaving Regions – Don't Forget Your Stuff*, discusses other uses of beacon technology and introduces functionalities based on when a user leaves a region. This chapter will introduce you to the possibilities of the technology for home automation before showing how to develop an application that ensures you don't leave your keys or wallet at home.

*Chapter 7, Vendor SDKs – Buying and Configuring Beacons*, discusses some popular vendor implementations of iBeacon hardware and takes you through some of the vendor software development kits to build a beacon configuration tool using the Estimote SDK, as buying iBeacon hardware can be difficult. By the end of this chapter, you'll be armed and confident to go and buy beacons for your commercial implementation.

*Chapter 8, Advanced Tutorial – iBeacon Museum*, pulls everything together with a more advanced tutorial. The tutorial focuses on an imaginary museum, which has different exhibits and multiple displays within each of the exhibits. As the user travels around the museum, the information shown in the app changes to show information about the display that they are currently closest to. As the user travels around the museum, you can track the user's journey on an interactive website.

*Chapter 9, iBeacon Security – Understanding the Risks*, arms you with a complete idea of the security vulnerabilities that need consideration when building apps that use iBeacon. This chapter also dispels any myths around security that concern users and discusses ways to naturally request the security permissions in an app without scaring users.

# What you need for this book

For this book, you will be required to download Xcode on your Mac OS X machine.

In order to jump quickly into the tutorials, you will need to download the companion app, which allows your Mac machine to act as an iBeacon and contains all of the iBeacon profiles featured in the book.

Your Mac needs to have Bluetooth 4.0 (which most do), but if it doesn't, there's no need to worry, as you can pick up a Bluetooth 4.0 USB dongle for under $15, which will allow the companion app to work.

To see whether your Mac is Bluetooth 4.0 enabled, follow these steps:

1. Click on the menu.
2. Select About This Mac.
3. Click on the More Info button.
4. Click on the System Report button.
5. Select Bluetooth from the sidebar on the left, underneath Hardware.
6. Scan down the list of information until you find LMP Version.
7. If your Mac is equipped with Bluetooth 4.0, LMP Version will say 0x6. Anything lower than that is an older version of Bluetooth and will need a USB dongle.

*Preface*

# Who this book is for

This book is designed for new or experienced iOS developers who want to build solutions that interact with the world around them. The book doesn't require you to have any prior experience in developing apps using Xcode and iOS SDKs, but some familiarity would allow you to get going very quickly. The tutorials are designed to progressively build on your knowledge until you are armed with everything you need to build proximity-powered solutions.

# Conventions

In this book, you will find a number of text styles that distinguish between different kinds of information. Here are some examples of these styles and an explanation of their meaning.

Code words in text, database table names, folder names, filenames, file extensions, pathnames, dummy URLs, user input, and Twitter handles are shown as follows: "In order to do this, we need to add a reference to `CoreLocation`."

A block of code is set as follows:

```
-(void)locationManager:(CLLocationManager *)manager
  didEnterRegion:(CLRegion *)region {
    UIAlertView * av = [[UIAlertView alloc] init];
    av.title = [NSString stringWithFormat:@"Entered Region
      '%@'", region.identifier];
    [av addButtonWithTitle:@"OK"];
    [av show];
}
```

Any command-line input or output is written as follows:

```
open Estimote\ Beacon\ Manager.xcworkspace/
```

**New terms** and **important words** are shown in bold. Words that you see on the screen, for example, in menus or dialog boxes, appear in the text like this: "Select **About This Mac**."

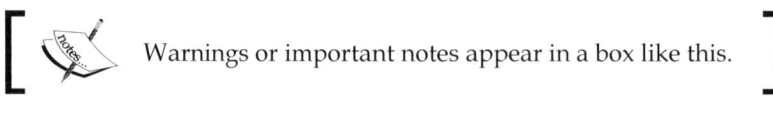
Warnings or important notes appear in a box like this.

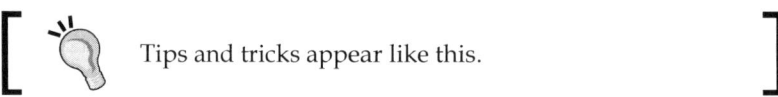
Tips and tricks appear like this.

[ 4 ]

# Reader feedback

Feedback from our readers is always welcome. Let us know what you think about this book—what you liked or disliked. Reader feedback is important for us as it helps us develop titles that you will really get the most out of.

To send us general feedback, simply e-mail feedback@packtpub.com, and mention the book's title in the subject of your message.

If there is a topic that you have expertise in and you are interested in either writing or contributing to a book, see our author guide at www.packtpub.com/authors.

# Customer support

Now that you are the proud owner of a Packt book, we have a number of things to help you to get the most from your purchase.

# Downloading the example code

You can download the example code files from your account at http://www.packtpub.com for all the Packt Publishing books you have purchased. If you purchased this book elsewhere, you can visit http://www.packtpub.com/support and register to have the files e-mailed directly to you.

# Errata

Although we have taken every care to ensure the accuracy of our content, mistakes do happen. If you find a mistake in one of our books—maybe a mistake in the text or the code—we would be grateful if you could report this to us. By doing so, you can save other readers from frustration and help us improve subsequent versions of this book. If you find any errata, please report them by visiting http://www.packtpub.com/submit-errata, selecting your book, clicking on the **Errata Submission Form** link, and entering the details of your errata. Once your errata are verified, your submission will be accepted and the errata will be uploaded to our website or added to any list of existing errata under the Errata section of that title.

To view the previously submitted errata, go to https://www.packtpub.com/books/content/support and enter the name of the book in the search field. The required information will appear under the **Errata** section.

## Piracy

Piracy of copyrighted material on the Internet is an ongoing problem across all media. At Packt, we take the protection of our copyright and licenses very seriously. If you come across any illegal copies of our works in any form on the Internet, please provide us with the location address or website name immediately so that we can pursue a remedy.

Please contact us at `copyright@packtpub.com` with a link to the suspected pirated material.

We appreciate your help in protecting our authors and our ability to bring you valuable content.

## Questions

If you have a problem with any aspect of this book, you can contact us at `questions@packtpub.com`, and we will do our best to address the problem.

# 1
# Welcome to iBeacon

Welcome to iBeacon—a range of opportunity! Back in the summer of 2013, Craig Federighi, Apple's Senior Vice President of Software Engineering, quietly announced that iOS 7 would feature iBeacon and ended months of speculation about when iOS devices would feature **Near Field Communication** (**NFC**)—the answer was that they didn't.

During the conference, Craig touched on why Apple devices wouldn't feature NFC when he discussed the new sharing features of **AirDrop**. He said, "There's no need to wander around the room bumping your phone with others." This, in a nutshell, shows the reason behind choosing iBeacon technology and the amazing commercial potential versus the limitations of the NFC technology, as iBeacon's range massively exceeds that of NFC.

## Introducing iBeacon

Simply put, an iBeacon is a **Bluetooth low energy** (**BLE**) device that emits a signal that conforms to the iBeacon specification. The iOS 7 SDK includes updates to the **Core Location** and **Core Bluetooth** frameworks that will allow you to build apps that respond to iBeacon signals or even act as an iBeacon transmitter.

The iBeacon specification for building hardware beacons is only available under nondisclosure agreement to vendors who sign up to the **Made for iPhone** (**MFi**) program. However, as an iOS developer, you don't need to know how to build hardware, you only need to understand how to interact with iBeacons or to simulate them with an iOS device, all of which we will cover in this book.

BLE is a groundbreaking leap in classic Bluetooth technology that allows the development of devices that can broadcast a signal up to 100 m (330 ft) with very little power consumption. This means that beacons can be produced for as little as $ 5 and broadcast for up to 2 years on a single lithium watch battery.

*Welcome to iBeacon*

# Hey, 'sup

There's often a misconception about what information an iBeacon can broadcast. Basically, an iBeacon broadcasts its presence and nothing more. It says, "Hey, here I am", and nothing else. You can't broadcast data using iBeacon technology, and similarly, iBeacons aren't snooping into where you're going or where you've been. Any data that your apps require outside of the iBeacon identification must be retrieved from another source such as a bundled database or cloud service, as shown in the following diagram:

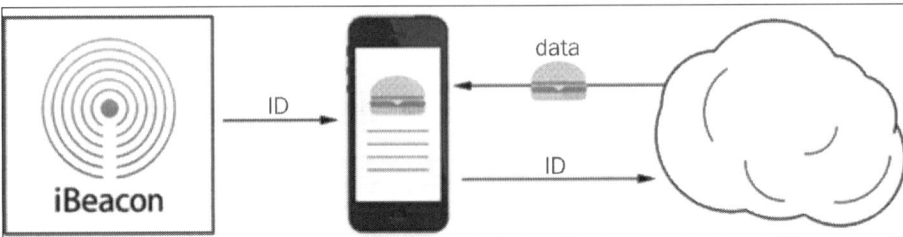

iBeacon app relationship

The best way to think about iBeacons is as a trigger for your app functionality. The trigger is based on the presence of a beacon or the relative distance of an iBeacon from your device.

iBeacons broadcast three values to help you identify which beacon your app is seeing. I call this the UUID/major/minor broadcasting triplet, discussed as follows:

- **UUID**: The **Universally Unique Identifier (UUID)** is application-specific and belongs only to your app and nobody else. You generate a UUID and tell your app to look out for this value and act accordingly when you come across an iBeacon broadcasting this value. It's specific to your app deployment and use case.
- **Major**: The major value further specifies a specific iBeacon and use case. For example, this could be the city that the beacon resides in or the actual store itself.
- **Minor**: The minor value allows further subdivision of the use case. For example, it could be the department within a store or a particular area of a theme park.

 By generating a UUID yourself, you ensure that nobody else can be using your UUID by accident. However, there isn't any governing body to register the use of a UUID with specific apps, so just be aware that people can spoof this value.

The following table shows how this UUID/major/minor triplet might be used by Disney to develop a queue-jumping app at some of their Walt Disney parks and resorts:

| Resort location | | Florida | California | Paris |
|---|---|---|---|---|
| UUID | | D03CA503-04B9-4D03-ABCE-54C9708A8C49 | | |
| Major | | 1 | 2 | 3 |
| Minor | Terror Tower | 10 | 10 | 10 |
| | Space Mountain | 20 | 20 | 20 |
| | Monorail | 30 | 30 | 30 |

A single multinational Disney resort's queue-jumping app could be used to determine your location and book your slot on the ride, provided you were located within the iBeacon proximity. As you can see from the preceding table, no information is passed to the device about the park or the ride itself; this information needs to be ascertained by the app from a different source such as a local database or cloud API before triggering the functionality based on that ride.

# Understanding a range using RSSI

Obviously, one of the most important factors that your app needs to be able to understand is the distance of mobile devices from the beacon itself. We'll cover this in depth in *Chapter 4, Ranging Beacons – Hunting for Treasure*, when we'll build a treasure hunt app that relies on the range of the beacon. For now, it's important to know that there's one extra piece of information that is broadcasted by iBeacons.

iBeacons broadcast one extra byte of data known as **measured power**. Measured power is a value representing the **received strength signal indication** (**RSSI**) value at a distance of 1 meter. RSSI is measured in dBm and indicates the measurable signal strength of the beacon, which decreases with distance. This RSSI value varies across the vendor beacon implementations and so isn't very reliable to determine the distance. This is where measured power comes into play.

When iBeacon vendors are configuring their hardware iBeacons, it's important that they configure the measured power broadcast value accurately because the Core Location framework uses this value to determine the distance of the beacon and converts it into a distance that you, as a developer, can utilize.

*Welcome to iBeacon*

> Think of the measured power value as a way of making an otherwise unreliable source of distance measuring reliable. In essence, it's a translation value that you don't see as a developer, but it's important for you to understand its value.

## Compatible devices

Although Apple only released the specification for BLE devices to broadcast iBeacon signals at the end of 2013, they'd been cleverly putting Bluetooth 4.0 hardware into devices since 2011, which means that even some older devices worked immediately with iBeacon with the release of iOS 7.

The following table lists some of the iBeacon-compatible iOS devices:

| Device family | Model | Release date |
|---|---|---|
| iPhone | iPhone 4s | October 14, 2011 |
| | iPhone 5 | September 21, 2012 |
| | iPhone 5s | September 20, 2013 |
| | iPhone 5c | September 20, 2013 |
| iPad | iPad Mini (first generation) | November 2, 2012 |
| | iPad Mini (second generation) | June 30, 2014 |
| | iPad (third generation) | March 16, 2012 |
| | iPad (fourth generation) | November 2, 2012 |
| | iPad Air | November 1, 2013 |
| iPod Touch | iPod Touch (fifth generation) | October 11, 2012 |

> Although not covered in this book, it's worth noting that Bluetooth beacons also work with Android devices that have Bluetooth 4.0 and running Android 4.3 and later, which includes some of the most popular devices (Samsung Galaxy S3/S4/S5/S4 Mini, Samsung Galaxy Note 2/3, HTC One, Google/LG Nexus 7 (2013 version)/Nexus 4/Nexus 5, and HTC Butterfly).

# Commercial applications of iBeacon

The commercial opportunities for iBeacon are endless. By adopting BLE, Apple have essentially brought location-based technology indoors and signed iOS devices up to the Internet of Things.

By formalizing a specification for the BLE technology for vendors and developers alike, Apple has essentially brought location- and proximity-based functionality indoors, which has obviously excited the home-automation community a great deal. However, it's the commercial app potential that excites most developers. The ability to understand, within a few feet, exactly where an iOS device is within a store, museum, or theme park means that we, as app developers, have been given a great big golden ticket of opportunity.

In December 2013, Apple leveraged iBeacon themselves by installing beacons in all 254 of their U.S. stores to become their very own case study. The Apple Store leveraged micro-location awareness to provide customers who had the official Apple Store app installed on their devices with information relevant to the items they were actually looking at.

Since Apple's iBeacon implementation, there have been a whole host of high-profile commercial projects, including:

- **Macy's** (http://bit.ly/macysibeacon): Macy's was the first major retailer to support iBeacon, which gives shoppers special offers and deals and rewards shoppers for their visits
- **Virgin Atlantic** (http://bit.ly/virgin-ibeacon): Virgin Atlantic has deployed iBeacons into London's Heathrow airport to give promotional offers while passengers are visiting the terminal
- **Major League Baseball** (http://bit.ly/mlb-ibeacon): Many Major League Baseball teams have now adopted iBeacons in stadiums to engage with fans on their mobile devices while at the game
- **Antwerp Museum** (http://bit.ly/antwerp-ibeacon): The Antwerp Museum has brought its exhibits to life with iBeacon, allowing visitors to move around its Rubens House exhibit and trigger information about the current display based on the user's current location

These are just some of the actual iBeacon implementations that are available at the time of writing this book. As far as your own projects go, the sky is the limit. Here are a few ideas to whet your appetite:

- **Proximity marketing**. Offer complete customized marketing when a customer enters your store combined with information about their previous purchases. As they pass some fine leather brogues say, "Hey, those blue leather brogues would look great with that floral shirt you bought last week."

- **Home automation**: Imagine pulling up to your drive and your porch lights turn on. That's not groundbreaking really; we've had movement sensors for years. However, imagine that the movement sensors, as well as turning your lights on, also started running you a bath, dimming the lights, and playing some relaxing music.
- **Museum exhibits**: Just like a personalized audio tour on your phone as you browse between exhibits and galleries without a predetermined direction, museum curators can build heatmaps of their most popular exhibits and reorganize galleries based on visitor behavior.
- **Venue navigation**: Get geofenced navigation of large venues with a custom tour guide app.
- **Conference interaction**: Using iBeacon, we could deliver location-context information and features. During a keynote your app could deliver features to people who are sitting in the theater, not to those walking around the exhibits outside the theater.
- **Car rental**: Just before you get on a flight, you could order and pay for your car rental. Then, when you arrive at the airport, your car could automatically unlock when you get near to it. This would require a little more computation and extra hardware within the car, but the essence is made possible by iBeacon.
- **Taxi alert**: Order a cab through your phone and receive a push notification when they're outside waiting for you.

# So many vendors, so little time

You've bought this book, so I'm going to don my super-sleuth hat and say that you've either been tasked with building an iOS app that utilizes iBeacon, or you've got a project in mind that would benefit from proximity-based location. Ignoring my limited powers of deduction, I'd say that's great news. This book will arm you with all the development knowledge you need to build any iBeacon-enabled iPhone and iPad apps. What the book won't give you though is some lovely iBeacon hardware.

Don't worry; you don't actually need any hardware to complete the tutorials in the book. This book includes an accompanying OS X app, which allows your Mac to become any beacon you want. I'll take you through getting it working later in this chapter.

If you're going to build a commercial application, you'll need to make a decision about which beacons to buy. I've been an early adopter of iBeacons and have sampled lots of the most popular beta devices, and so, hopefully, I can give you some insights into the different implementations of iBeacons between vendors.

At the time of writing this book, the process to become an iBeacon vendor was to sign up to the MFi program and gain the specifications for iBeacons. The ones I've sampled personally are motes from Estimote, RedBearLab's RedBear Beacon B1, and ROXIMITY beacons. Many vendors supply their own SDKs with their hardware, and we'll explore some of these SDKs in *Chapter 7, Vendor SDKs – Buying and Configuring Beacons*, but for now, we'll go through the main differences between the vendors' iBeacon implementations to help you make a more informed choice when it comes to sourcing hardware for your commercial project.

# Estimote

Have a look at the following figure that shows what motes look like:

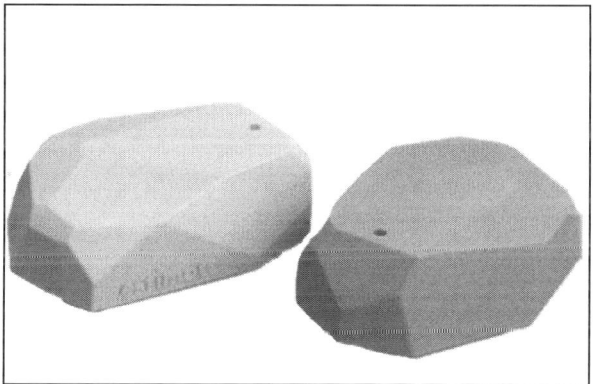

Estimote Beacons or motes

Estimote was set up with $ 3.1 million seed funding in December 2013 and have been well featured in digital press news stories, including the TechCrunch and Wired magazines. Their marketing material boasts that their motes can run up to 2 years on a single watch battery, and their stylish silicon casing means that they work beautifully outside too.

Estimote beacon sensors are already being used by large retailers in Europe, and they're working to build a large network of their sensors in the U.S.

Estimote has opted to provide a richer feature set than most beacons by including accelerometer hardware and temperature sensors. Although these sensors are only accessible when using the Estimote SDK, they do allow for a more creative set of projects to be developed.

Estimote has definitely ridden the crest of the tsunami of iBeacon technology in the press and has some very high-profile customers. At the time of writing this book, the beacons themselves were available as a $ 99 development kit containing three beacons and weren't available for larger volumes as a commercial purchase.

Estimote offers an SDK for managing and interacting with their beacons and has also provided an iOS app available in the App Store, which includes a number of development tutorials and tools such as:

- **Distance- and proximity-based demos**: This tool shows the distance of the device in meters or in written English (near, far, and so on) from Estimote beacons
- **Notifications demo**: This tool shows you a local push notification when you enter into the Estimote Beacon's region
- **Accelerometer and temperature sensor**: Beacons also include an accelerometer and temperature sensor for more imaginative projects to be developed
- **Beacon management**: This tool allows you to check the status of your Estimote beacons including battery life, temperature, and hardware settings, as well as allowing you to configure the beacon's UUID/major/minor broadcast triplet values

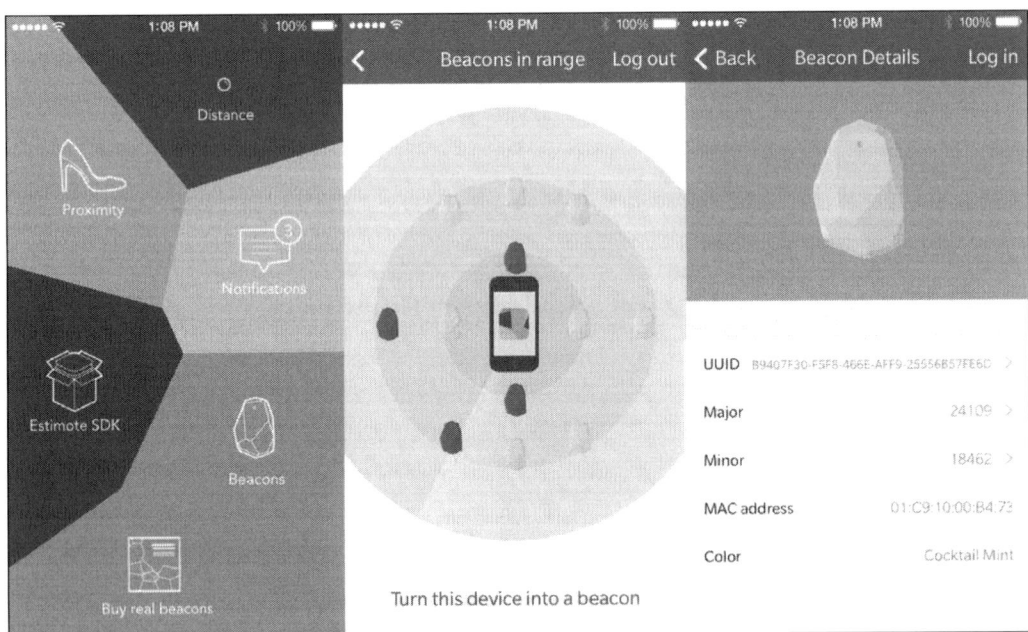

Some of the Estimote companion app's features

## Estimote beacons – pros

The following are some pros of Estimote beacons:

- They are beautifully designed, and so once released commercially, they have all the elegant aesthetics to feature immediately in any retail- or customer-facing environment
- They have good support for both iOS and Android applications using the Estimote SDK
- They have a silicon cover, which means that beacons can be used outside

## Estimote beacons – cons

The following are some cons of Estimote beacons:

- They are not yet commercially available, and you can only buy developer packs
- They have sealed silicon units, which means that battery replacement is likely to destroy the unit
- They have wait times of up to 6 weeks for developer kit availability

# ROXIMITY

ROXIMITY has taken a completely different approach and made their beacons completely centrally managed. There's no Bluetooth beacon configuration and beacons can be repurposed for multiple apps simultaneously. You *can* use a single ROXIMITY beacon within an app dedicated to a shopping mall for direction and also for a loyalty app of a retail store within the mall itself because they don't use the UUID/major/minor broadcasting triplet. These values have been removed from you as a developer when using ROXIMITY beacons. Instead, you can work with ROXIMITY beacon identifiers and *must* use the ROXIMITY SDK; you can't use the Core Location framework.

> *"The ROXIMITY Beacon hardware and software are designed and built for large-scale deployments. Our beacons are designed for easy installation and zero maintenance."*
>
> *- http://roximity.com/platform/*

The ROXIMITY beacons and hardware are most definitely geared up for mobile marketing, and so may not be the best choice for highly customized functionality. However, if your goal is to provide ROXIMITY-based marketing to specialist apps such as sporting venues, shopping malls, or airports, then ROXIMITY beacons and the SDK are probably the most comprehensive beacons to use straight out of the box.

*Welcome to iBeacon*

ROXIMITY features are all centrally managed via the online merchant dashboard. By following ROXIMITY's approach to beacon management, you, as a solutions provider, would need to complete the following steps to deploy beacons at your target location:

1. Buy ROXIMITY beacons from the ROXIMITY website.
2. Beacons are shipped to you and added to your online merchant dashboard.
3. Configure a new application on the merchant dashboard and choose which beacons will be attached to the application.
4. Add the ROXIMITY SDK to your app and wire up the delegate methods.

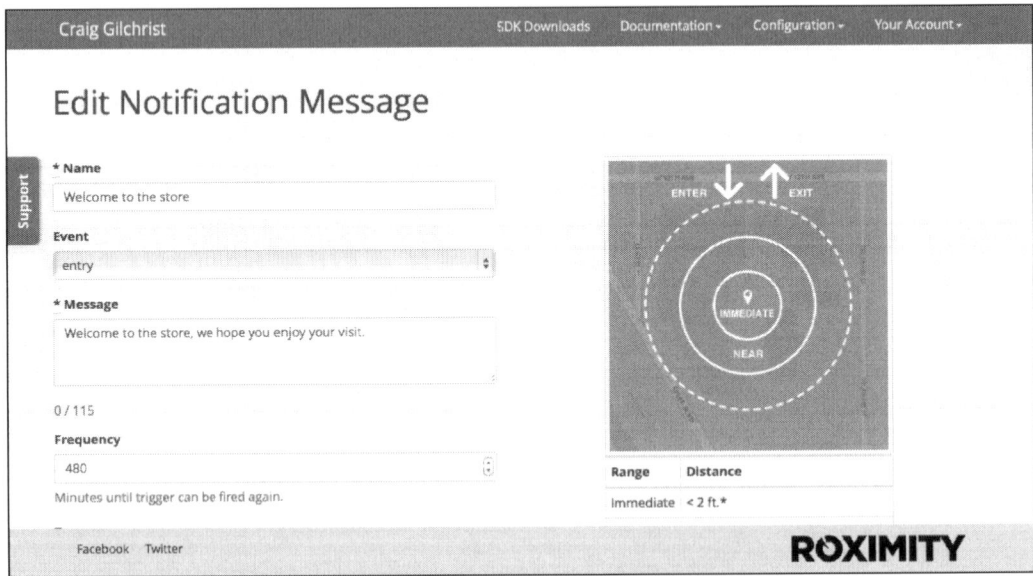

ROXIMITY merchant dashboard notification message dialog

By following this simple approach, you already have tons of features available without having to write a single line of custom code:

- ROXIMITY allows you to send push notifications directly via their merchant dashboard and configure push notifications.
- ROXIMITY provides in-depth analytics of visitors.
- The ROXIMITY SDK is capable of verifying a device's phone number for a user. Doing so provides additional reachability and location information for that user and an additional means to look up or request that user's location.

- The ROXIMITY SDK, when correctly implemented into your app, reports the exact location of your beacons placed in their commercial location. This exact location can also be configured using the ROXIMITY Beacon Explorer app that ROXIMITY offers via the App Store.
- Message dialogs can be configured to capture responses when users enter a region via the merchant dashboard.

> The ROXIMITY Beacon Explorer app (http://bit.ly/roximity-be) allows you to demonstrate and test your dialogs and settings without having to build the app using their SDK. This is great for testing functionality before you start building your app.

## ROXIMITY beacons – pros

The following are some pros of ROXIMITY beacons:

- Rapid development with an extensive SDK
- Single beacons can be used in multiple apps because they don't rely on the UUID/major/minor broadcasting triplet
- They have no hardware configuration requirements (via Bluetooth), meaning beacons can be quickly and easily reused for other purposes, and marketing campaigns can be optimized via a central management platform

## ROXIMITY beacons – cons

The following are some cons of ROXIMITY beacons:

- No control over the UUID/major/minor broadcasting triplet, and so the ROXIMITY SDK must be used, which means that the iOS SDK can't be used for development
- Too much emphasis on proximity marketing means that using ROXIMITY beacons for other purposes is more difficult than simpler beacon implementations
- Currently, only very limited analytics are available via the merchant dashboard

# RedBearLab

**RedBearLab** is a Hong-Kong-based company that specializes in BLE technology exclusively. They have many BLE products such as Arduino shields and have an established name in hardware.

The RedBear Beacon B1

RedBearLab adopted a simple, no-nonsense approach in their iBeacon product, the RedBear Beacon B1, and have focused on the hardware, not branding.

Much bigger than both the ROXIMITY and Estimote options, the RedBear Beacon B1 is powered by two AAA batteries, offering five times the battery life of beacons that are powered by a CR2032 coin battery.

RedBearLab don't provide any online management platform for their beacons; however, they do offer over-the-air firmware upgrades, which means that firmware updates can be easily done via their RedBear BeaconTool app available via the App Store (`http://bit.ly/RedBear-BT`).

The RedBear Beacon B1 also features very simple administration via the BeaconTool app and is very secure compared to other beacons since it has a hardware configuration button, which activates the configuration mode for a short period. Combining this hardware feature with the fact that you can very easily set custom administrator passwords on the beacon means that these devices are far less likely to be hijacked than other vendor beacons. We will discuss the security issues surrounding iBeacons in *Chapter 9, iBeacon Security – Understanding the Risks*.

Finally, the RedBear Beacon B1 has one unique feature that is both elegant and genius—a power switch. None of the other beacons I've had the pleasure of trialing have this feature, which when developing an app makes perfect sense. A hardware power switch allowing you to turn a beacon on and off makes simulating entering and exiting a beacon region very simple.

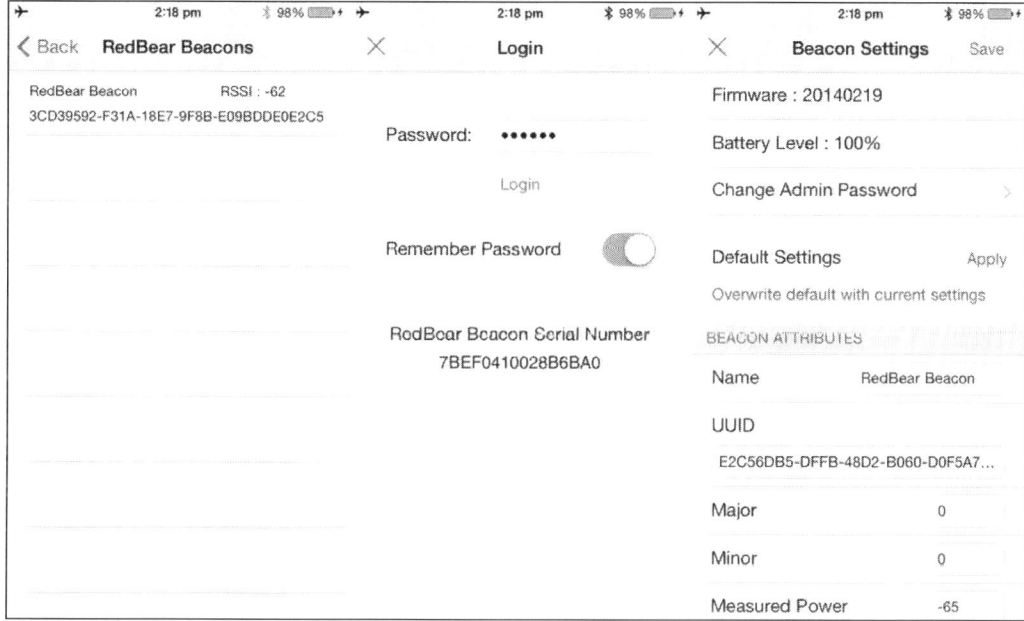

RedBear BeaconTool app for iOS

The RedBear Beacon B1 and RedBear BeaconTool app provide simple configuration, robust hardware security, and power features, which mean it's the perfect development companion.

## RedBear Beacon B1 – pros

The following are the pros of RedBear Beacon B1:

- Hardware button to switch between configuration and online mode, making it more difficult for unauthorized configuration of the UUID/major/minor broadcasting triplet
- Longest battery life and easiest unit to change batteries
- Power switch allows easy simulation of entering and existing beacon range

## RedBear Beacon B1 – cons

The following are the cons of RedBear Beacon B1:

- Largest beacon of the three discussed and heavy in comparison when including two AAA batteries.
- Aesthetically, this is the least pleasing of the beacons discussed. This means it is not great for consumer-facing commercial deployments.
- No extra sensors or software features present like the other two beacons discussed.

## Other vendor options

There are of course plenty of other vendors and more and more new beacons coming onto the market all the time, so there'll be lots of amazing new vendors for you to choose from.

The three discussed are just some of the most popular beacons that I've had the pleasure of testing and so can share my experiences. If you're buying beacons in bulk, then you might also want to consider using a trade website such as http://www.alibaba.com/. I've had some great beacons and some not so great beacons through this online trading platform, but overall, my experiences have been good. The three beacons we've already discussed range between $ 23 per unit and $ 35 per unit. However, when buying direct from suppliers on Alibaba.com, I've personally bought very good units for as little as $ 4 per unit.

When buying iBeacons from trade websites, my recommendation is that you order a subset first, maybe 5 to 10 units. Most vendors will charge you $ 2 to $ 3 more per unit for this type of transaction and offer you economies of scale for buying more in future.

When buying iBeacons from trade sites, you should also look out for beacons that have conformed to the Made for iPhone program; a key way of identifying these is when they show the iBeacon logo.

Made for iPhone logo

*Chapter 1*

# The companion OS X application and website

In order to complete the tutorials in this book, you don't need to be in possession of any iBeacon hardware since there's a companion app that lets your Mac act as an iBeacon using its built-in Bluetooth adapter provided it has Bluetooth 4.0.

You can download the companion app from the companion website as well as all of the code tutorials from the app. You can download the companion app and code samples from:

```
http://ibeacon.university/
```

If your machine doesn't have Bluetooth 4.0, there's no need to worry. You can pick up a Bluetooth 4.0 USB dongle for under $ 15 that will allow the companion app to work.

To see if your Mac is Bluetooth 4.0 enabled, follow these steps:

1. Click on the Apple icon in the status bar.
2. Select **About This Mac**.
3. Click on the **More Info** button.
4. Click on the **System Report** button.
5. Select **Bluetooth** from the sidebar on the left, underneath **Hardware**.
6. Scan down the list of information until you find **LMP Version**, as shown:

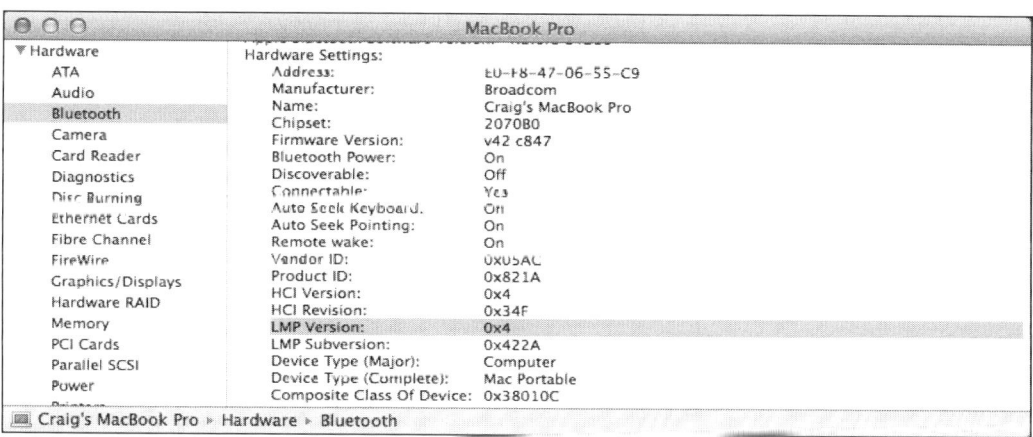

If your Mac is equipped with Bluetooth 4.0, LMP Version will say **0x6**. Anything lower than that is an older version of Bluetooth and will need a USB dongle.

[ 21 ]

*Welcome to iBeacon*

The Mac in the preceding screenshot needs a dongle.

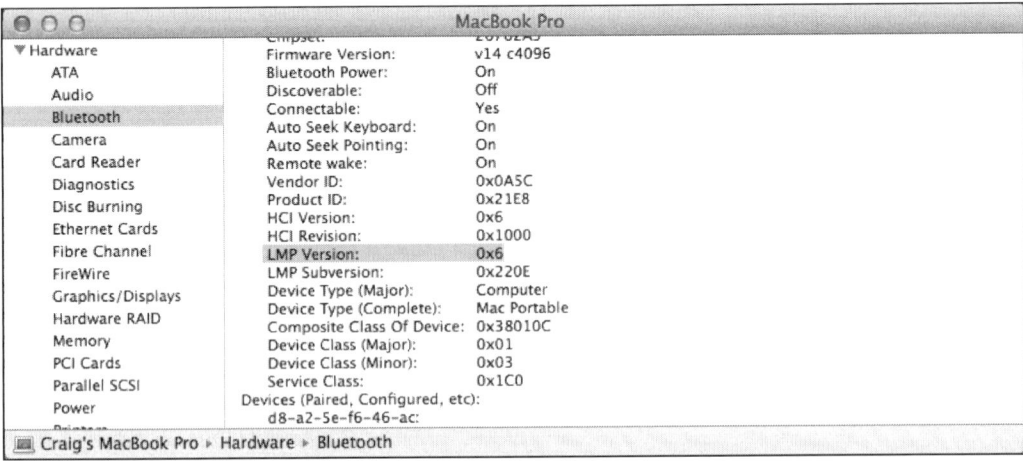

The earlier screenshot shows a MacBook Pro fitted with Bluetooth 3.1 and will need a USB dongle.

The Mac in the preceding screenshot shows the same MacBook Pro with a USB dongle fitted.

>  While writing this book, I used a MacBook Pro from late 2011, which unfortunately is only fitted with Bluetooth 3.1. I picked up a pluggable USB-BT4LE Bluetooth 4.0 USB Adapter for $ 13, which enabled my MacBook for iBeacon transmissions.

## Using the companion app

The companion app is used throughout the book and lets you use your Mac as an iBeacon. It can be downloaded from the download section of the Packt Publishing website and comes preconfigured with all of the beacons used throughout the book.

Chapter 1

Using the companion app, you can simulate physical beacons in the real world using any Bluetooth-4.0-powered Mac running OS X Mavericks or Mountain Lion.

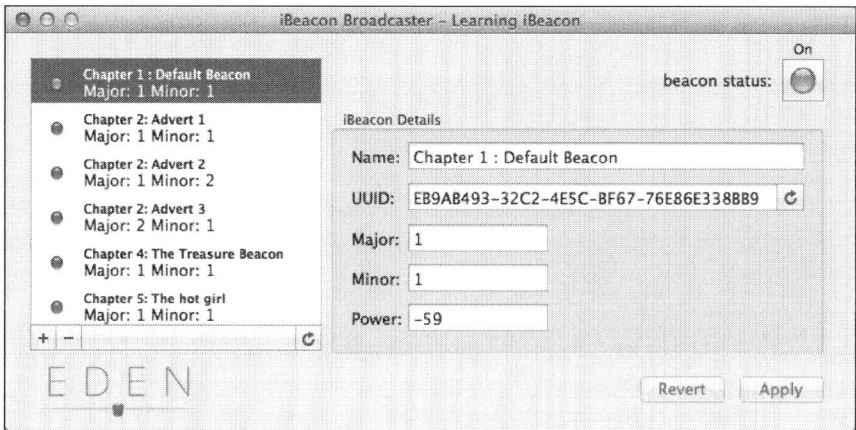

Companion app broadcasting an iBeacon signal

The companion OS X app has beacons configured already for every tutorial in this book. To start a beacon, simply select the beacon from the tutorial from the menu on the left, and then tap on the power button in the right panel.

The features of the companion app can be seen in the following table:

| Button | Use |
| --- | --- |
| + | Add new iBeacon profiles to suit your own development needs using the add button |
| - | Remove iBeacon profiles using the minus button |
| ⟳ | If you lose some of the tutorial beacons, then reset the app iBeacon profiles using the reset button |

# Hello world

In time-honored tradition, we can't conclude the first chapter without the traditional "Hello World" tutorial. We'll be using your Mac as an iBeacon broadcaster using the companion app, and the app will simply show an alert every time it enters or exits the region.

*Welcome to iBeacon*

We will cover all of these concepts in more detail in later chapters, but for reference, here are the classes we'll be using:

- `CLLocationManager`: The `CLLocationManager` class delivers location-related events to your app and tells you when you enter or exit a region
- `CLLocationManagerDelegate`: The `CLLocationManagerDelegate` protocol defines the delegate methods used to receive location and heading updates from `CLLocationManager`
- `CLBeaconRegion`: A `CLBeaconRegion` object defines a type of region that is based on the device's proximity to a Bluetooth beacon

# Let's get started

Fire up Xcode and start a new project. Choose **Single View Application** from the iOS template menu as your project type.

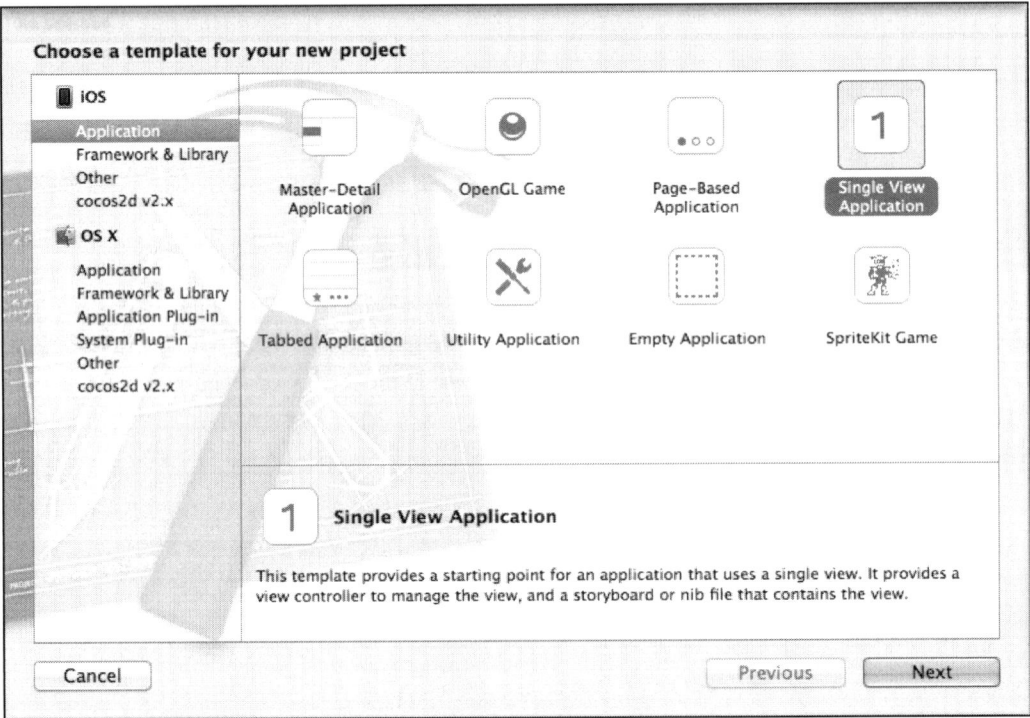

A new project dialog

Set up your new project using the values shown in the following screenshot:

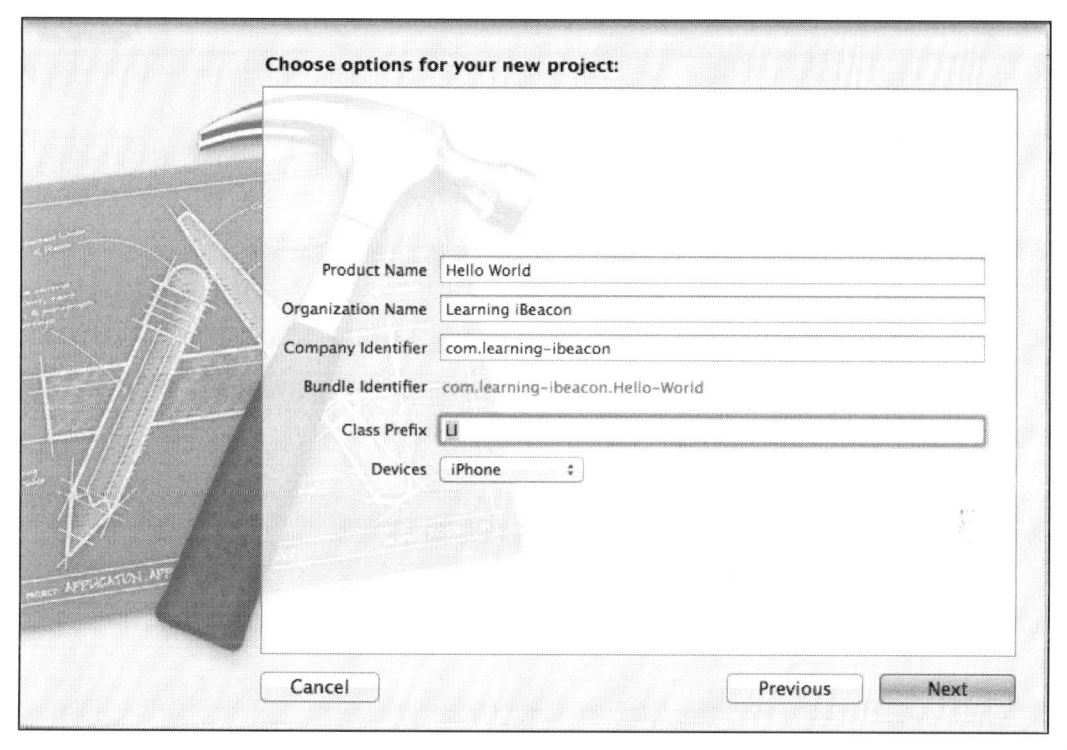

*A new project options dialog*

# Adding the Core Location framework

All of the features we need for this app to work are present in the Core Location framework.

*Welcome to iBeacon*

Click on the project in the project navigator and scroll down to the **Linked Frameworks and Libraries** section of the **General** tab and then click on the add icon. We'll need to add the `CoreLocation` framework as shown in the following screenshot:

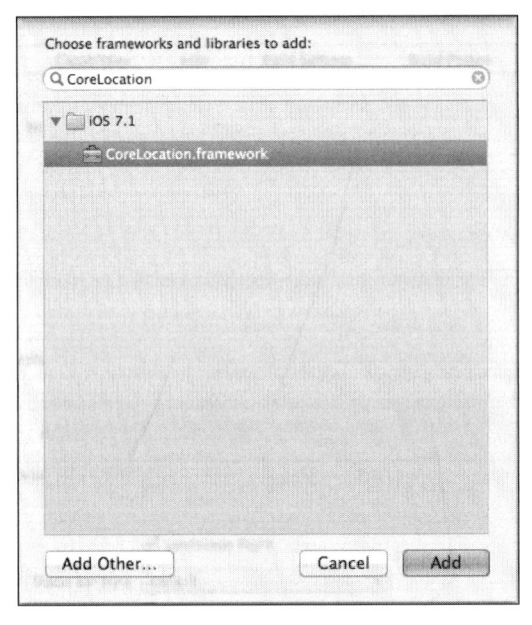

Adding the Core Location framework

We only really care about the `LIViewController` class for this tutorial as that's where we're going to be presenting to the user when we're moving in and out of regions. In order to do this, we need to add a reference to `CoreLocation`. Open `LIViewController.h` and add the following line just below the existing `UIKit` import:

```
#import <CoreLocation/CoreLocation.h>
```

> **Downloading the example code**
>
> You can download the example code files for all Packt books you have purchased from your account at http://www.packtpub.com. If you purchased this book elsewhere, you can visit http://www.packtpub.com/support and register to have the files e-mailed directly to you.

# Adding a permission message

Since iOS 8.0, you *must* specify a location description message in your plist settings. This is a nice friendly message for the users to help them understand why they need permission to use those location services. To do this, open the project file, click on your target **Hello World**, and then under the **Info** tab, add a new item to the dictionary under **Custom iOS Target Properties** with the following values:

- **Key**: `NSLocationAlwaysUsageDescription`
- **Value**: `This app needs your location to show you how cool iBeacon is.`

# Configuring the CLLocationManagerDelegate method

Our `ViewController` instance is where all the action happens, so it makes sense for `ViewController` to be aware of location events. For that, we need to make it `CLLocationManagerDelegate`.

Go ahead and add the declaration to the `LIViewController` interface declaration. Change the interface declaration in `LIViewController.h` so that it looks like the following code:

```
@interface LIViewController :
  UIViewController<CLLocationManagerDelegate>
```

We also need to implement the `CLLocationManagerDelegate` methods so that we can show our notification when the device enters a region. Add the following code to the end of the `LIViewController` implementation in the `LIViewController.m` file:

```
-(void)locationManager:(CLLocationManager *)manager
   didEnterRegion:(CLRegion *)region {
     UIAlertView * av = [[UIAlertView alloc] init];
     av.title = [NSString stringWithFormat:@"Entered Region
       '%@'", region.identifier];
     [av addButtonWithTitle:@"OK"];
     [av show];
}

-(void)locationManager:(CLLocationManager *)manager
   didExitRegion:(CLRegion *)region {
     UIAlertView * av = [[UIAlertView alloc] init];
     av.title = [NSString stringWithFormat:@"Left Region
       '%@'", region.identifier];
```

*Welcome to iBeacon*

```
    [av addButtonWithTitle:@"OK"];
    [av show];
}
```

> "Wait, what's CLRegion?" I hear you asking. Well, CLBeaconRegion inherits CLRegion and so CLBeaconRegion *is* CLRegion. Remember that CLLocationManager is used to deliver location-related events, which don't necessarily need to come from a beacon-related activity.

## Adding a CLLocationManager instance

Now, our view controller will be notified when a CLLocationManager instance receives events, but we don't have an instance of CLLocationManager yet. Add the following property to the LIViewController interface inside LIViewController.m:

```
@property (nonatomic, strong) CLLocationManager * locationManager;
```

## Preparing UUID

For our app to know which region it's looking out for, we need some way of storing the UUID. Add the following line just below the implementation in LIViewController.m:

```
static NSString * uuid = @"EB9AB493-32C2-4E5C-BF67-76E86E338BB9";
```

## Start monitoring

Our app is already ready to start accepting location-based updates. All we need to do now is create a region, instantiate our location manager, and start monitoring our regions. Overwrite the viewDidLoad method of our LIViewController with the following code. We'll go through the most important code shortly.

```
- (void)viewDidLoad
{
    [super viewDidLoad];
    NSUUID * regionUUID = [[NSUUID alloc]
      initWithUUIDString:uuid];

    CLBeaconRegion * region = [[CLBeaconRegion alloc]
      initWithProximityUUID:regionUUID identifier:@"My Region"];

    [region setNotifyOnEntry:YES];
    [region setNotifyOnExit:YES];
```

```
    self.locationManager = [[CLLocationManager alloc] init];
    self.locationManager.delegate = self;

    [self.locationManager requestAlwaysAuthorization];

    [self.locationManager startMonitoringForRegion:region];
}
```

# Line by line

Let's break the preceding code down line by line:

1. First, we create an NSUUID instance using our string identifier (uuid) since CLBeaconRegion requires an object of this type in order to be initialized:

   ```
   NSUUID * regionUUID = [[NSUUID alloc]
     initWithUUIDString:uuid];
   ```

2. Next, we create a new CLBeaconRegion passing in our NSUUID:

   ```
   CLBeaconRegion * region = [[CLBeaconRegion alloc]
     initWithProximityUUID:regionUUID
     identifier:@"My Region"];
   ```

3. Next, we configure our region events. We're interested in being notified when we enter and leave the region:

   ```
   [region setNotifyOnEntry:YES];
   [region setNotifyOnExit:YES];
   ```

4. Next, we instantiate CLLocationManager and add ViewController as its delegate:

   ```
   self.locationManager = [[CLLocationManager alloc] init];
   self.locationManager.delegate = self;
   ```

5. Finally, we request permission for location services, then start monitoring for the CLBeaconRegion we've just created:

   ```
   [self.locationManager requestAlwaysAuthorization];
   [self.locationManager startMonitoringForRegion:region];
   ```

*Welcome to iBeacon*

# Testing our code

Plug in an iOS device to your Mac, and compile and debug the app. You should be presented with a lovely blank white screen. Because we're using `CoreLocation`, you need to give permission for the app to use your location. It's important that you agree to this:

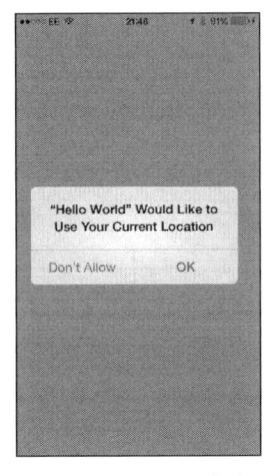

Location permission dialog

Now, open the companion app on your Mac and choose the beacon profile named **Chapter 1 : Default Beacon** from the list on the left-hand side and then click on the power button, as shown in the following screenshot:

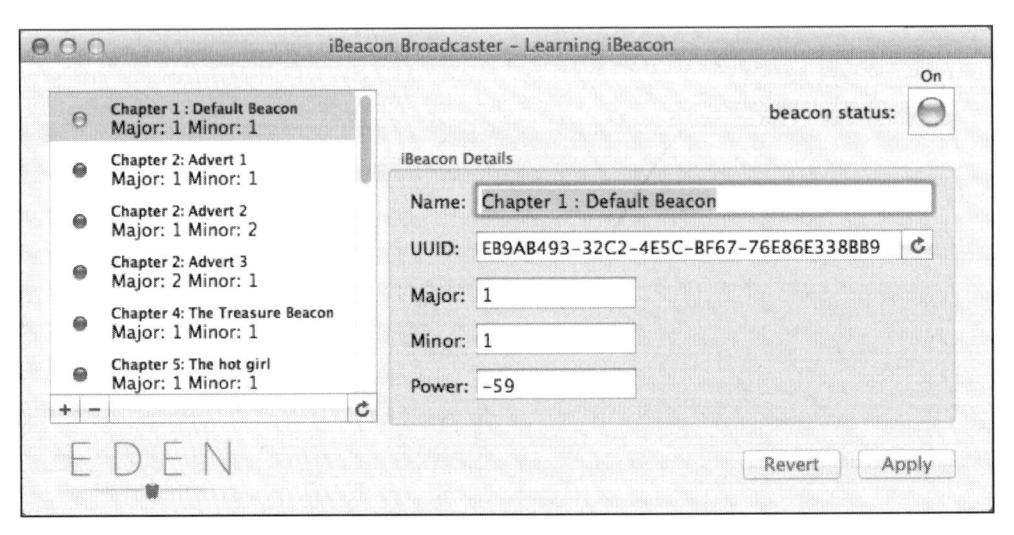

Using your Mac to broadcast your first iBeacon

*Chapter 1*

What you've just simulated is your device entering a region. If this was a real scenario, the beacon would have been running all along and your device would come into range because you walk towards the beacon, but the companion app serves just as well in this instance.

If all was successful, you should see the following screenshot:

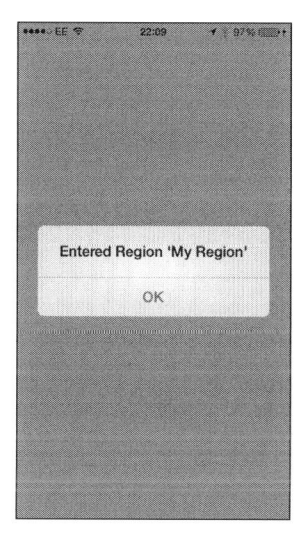

Successfully entered the region

Finally, test exiting the region by turning the beacon profile off in the companion OS X app. It may take up to 30 seconds for the app to register that you've left the region. Once the event fires, you should see the following screenshot:

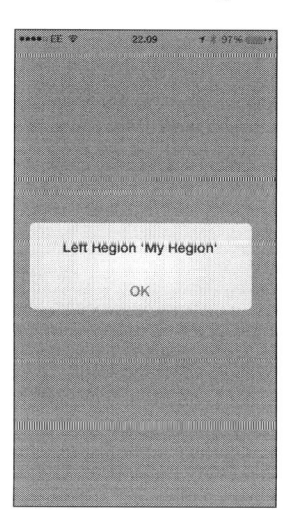

Successfully exited the region

> The reason for the delay is that the `didExitRegion` method is meant for tidying up resources after ranging beacons, which we'll cover in the later chapters. Apple's implementation includes a delay to ensure the event isn't fired when the Bluetooth signal may be subject to interference.

# Summary

Congratulations on building your first app using iBeacon technology! You've added the first building blocks to your arsenal of tools to build amazing indoor location-based applications. The rest of the book concentrates less on the technology and more on the code, and next we'll be covering more in-depth functionality by showing proximity-based marketing. Hold on to your hats!

# 2
# Detecting Beacons – Showing an Advert

In the previous chapter, we introduced you to the amazing possibilities of iBeacon and brought the UUID/major/minor broadcasting triplet to your attention. We also built our first, albeit very simple, app that detected the presence of beacons.

In this chapter, we're going to expand our knowledge and get an in-depth understanding of the broadcasting triplet, and we'll expand on some of the important classes within the Core Location framework.

To help demonstrate the more in-depth concepts, we'll build an app that shows different advertisements depending on the major and minor values of the beacon that it detects. We'll be using the context of an imaginary department store called Matey's. Matey's are currently undergoing iBeacon trials in their flagship London store and at the moment are giving offers on their different-themed restaurants and also on their ladies clothing to users who are using their branded app.

## Uses of the UUID/major/minor broadcasting triplet

In the last chapter, we covered the reasons behind the broadcasting triplet; we're going to use the triplet with a more realistic scenario. Let's go over the three values again in some more detail.

### UUID – Universally Unique Identifier

The UUID is meant to be unique to your app. It can be spoofed, which we'll cover in *Chapter 9, iBeacon Security – Understanding the Risks*, but generally, your app would be the only app looking for that UUID.

*Detecting Beacons – Showing an Advert*

The UUID identifies a region, which is the maximum broadcast range of a beacon from its center point. Think of a region as a circle of broadcast with the beacon in the middle.

If lots of beacons with the same UUID have overlapping broadcasting ranges, then the region is represented by the broadcasting range of all the beacons combined as shown in the following figure. The combined range of all the beacons with the same UUID becomes the region.

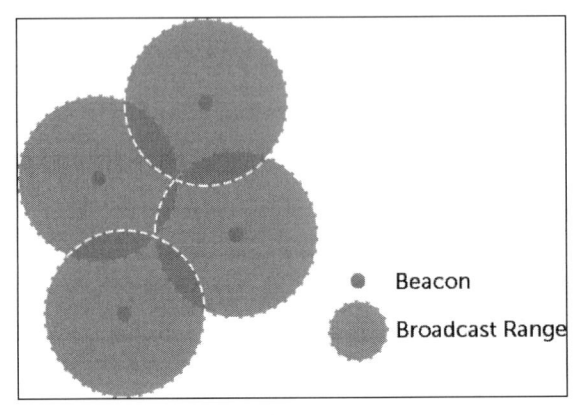

Broadcast range

More specifically, the region is represented by an instance of the `CLBeaconRegion` class, which we'll cover in more detail later in this chapter. The following code shows how to configure `CLBeaconRegion`:

```
NSString * uuidString = @"78BC6634-A424-4E05-A2AE-A59A25CAC4A9";

NSUUID * regionUUID;
regionUUID = [[NSUUID alloc] initWithUUIDString:uuidString"];

CLBeaconRegion * region;
region = [[CLBeaconRegion alloc] initWithProximityUUID:
    regionUUID identifier:@"My Region"];
```

Generally, most apps will be monitoring only for one region. This is normally sufficient since the major and minor values are 16-bit unsigned integers, which means that each value can be a number up to 65,535 giving 4,294,836,225 unique beacon combinations per UUID.

Since the major and minor values are used to represent a subsection of the use case, there may be a time when 65,535 combinations of a major value may not be enough and so, this would be the rare time that your app can monitor multiple regions with different UUIDs. Another more likely example is that your app has multiple use cases, which are more logically split by UUID.

An example where an app has multiple use cases would be a loyalty app that has offers for many different retailers when the app is within the vicinity of the retail stores. Here you can have a different UUID for every retailer.

# Major

The major value further identifies your use case. The major value should separate your use case along logical categories. This could be sections in a shopping mall or exhibits in a museum. In our example, a use case of the major value represents the different types of service within a department store.

In some cases, you may wish to separate logical categories into more than one major value. This would only be if each category has more than 65,535 beacons.

# Minor

The minor value ultimately identifies the beacon itself. If you consider the major value as the category, then the minor value is the beacon within that category.

# An example of a use case

The example laid out in this chapter uses the following UUID/major/minor values to broadcast different adverts for Matey's:

| Department | | Food | Women's clothing |
|---|---|---|---|
| UUID | | 8F0C1DDC 11E5 1A07 8910 125941B072F9 ||
| Major | | 1 | 2 |
| Minor | 1 | 30 percent off on sushi at The Japanese Kitchen | 50 percent off on all ladies' clothing |
| | 2 | Buy one get one free at Tucci's Pizza | N/A |

# Understanding Core Location

The Core Location framework lets you determine the current location or heading associated with the device. The framework has been around since 2008 and was present in iOS 2.0. Up until the release of iOS 7, the framework was only used for geolocation based on GPS coordinates and so was suitable only for outdoor location.

The framework got a new set of classes and new methods were added to the existing classes to accommodate the beacon-based location functionality. Let's explore a few of these classes in more detail.

## The CLBeaconRegion class

Geo-fencing (geofencing) is a feature in a software program that uses the **global positioning system** (**GPS**) or **radio frequency identification** (**RFID**) to define geographical boundaries. A geofence is a virtual barrier.

The CLBeaconRegion class defines a geofenced boundary identified by a UUID and the collective range of all physical beacons with the same UUID. When a device matching the CLBeaconRegion UUID comes in range, the region triggers the delivery of an appropriate notification.

CLBeaconRegion inherits CLRegion, which also serves as the superclass of CLCircularRegion. The CLCircularRegion class defines the location and boundaries for a circular geographic region. You can use instances of this class to define geofences for a specific location, but it shouldn't be confused with CLBeaconRegion. The CLCircularRegion class shares many of the same methods but is specifically related to a geographic location based on the GPS coordinates of the device. The following figure shows the CLRegion class and its descendants.

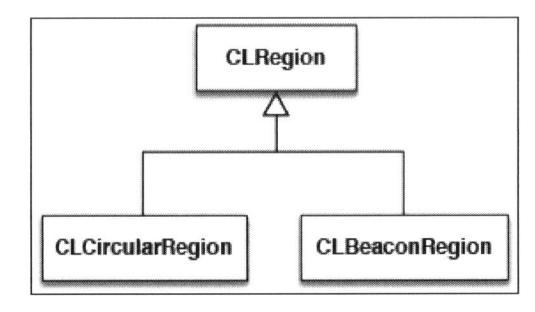

The CLRegion class hierarchy

## The CLLocationManager class

The `CLLocationManager` class defines the interface for configuring the delivery of location-and heading-related events to your application. You use an instance of this class to establish the parameters that determine when location and heading events should be delivered and to start and stop the actual delivery of those events. You can also use a location manager object to retrieve the most recent location and heading data.

## Creating a CLLocationManager class

The `CLLocationManager` class is used to track both geolocation and proximity based on beacons. To start tracking beacon regions using the `CLLocationManager` class, we need to do the following:

1. Create an instance of `CLLocationManager`.
2. Assign an object conforming to the `CLLocationManagerDelegate` protocol to the delegate property.
3. Call the appropriate start method to begin the delivery of events.

All location- and heading-related updates are delivered to the associated delegate object, which is a custom object that you provide.

## Defining a CLLocationManager class line by line

Consider the following steps to define a `CLLocationManager` class line by line:

1. Every class that needs to be notified about `CLLocationManager` events needs to first import the Core Location framework (usually in the header file) as shown:

    ```
    #import <CoreLocation/CoreLocation.h>
    ```

2. Then, once the framework is imported, the class needs to declare itself as implementing the `CLLocationManagerDelegate` protocol like the following view controller does:

    ```
    @interface MyViewController :
      UIViewController<CLLocationManagerDelegate>
    ```

*Detecting Beacons – Showing an Advert*

3. Next, you need to create an instance of `CLLocationManager` and set your class as the instance delegate of `CLLocationManager` as shown:

   ```
   CLLocationManager * locationManager =
     [[CLLocationManager alloc] init];
   locationManager.delegate = self;
   ```

4. You then need a region for your location manager to work with:

   ```
   // Create a unique ID to identify our region.
   NSUUID * regionId = [[NSUUID alloc]
     initWithUUIDString:@"
     AD32373E-9969-4889-9507-C89FCD44F94E"];

   // Create a region to monitor.
   CLBeaconRegion * beaconRegion =
     [[CLBeaconRegion alloc] initWithProximityUUID:
     regionId identifier:@"My Region"];
   ```

5. Finally, you need to call the appropriate start method using the beacon region. Each start method has a different purpose, which we'll explain shortly:

   ```
   // Start monitoring and ranging beacons.
   [locationManager startMonitoringForRegion:beaconRegion];
   [locationManager startRangingBeaconsInRegion:beaconRegion];
   ```

6. Once the class is imported, you need to implement the methods of the `CLLocationManagerDelegate` protocol.

Some of the most important delegate methods are explained shortly. This isn't an exhaustive list of the methods, but it does include all of the important methods we'll be using in this chapter. A complete list of the `CLLocationManagerDelegate` methods can be found on the Apple developer site:

https://developer.apple.com/library/ios/documentation/corelocation/reference/cllocationmanagerdelegate_protocol/index.html

## locationManager:didEnterRegion

Whenever you enter a region that your location manager has been instructed to look for (by calling `startRangingBeaconsInRegion`), the `locationManager:didEnterRegion` delegate method is called. This method gives you an opportunity to do something with the region such as start monitoring for specific beacons, shown as follows:

```
-(void)locationManager:(CLLocationManager *)
  manager didEnterRegion:(CLRegion *)region {
    // Do something when we enter a region.
}
```

## locationManager:didExitRegion

Similarly, when you exit the region, the `locationManager:didExitRegion` delegate method is called. Here you can do things like stop monitoring for specific beacons, shown as follows:

```
-(void)locationManager:(CLLocationManager *)manager
   didExitRegion:(CLRegion *)region {
      // Do something when we exit a region.
}
```

> When testing your region monitoring code on a device, realize that region events may not happen immediately after a region boundary is crossed. To prevent spurious notifications, iOS does not deliver region notifications until certain threshold conditions are met. Specifically, the user's location must cross the region boundary and move away from that boundary by a minimum distance and remain at that minimum distance for at least 20 seconds before the notifications are reported.

## locationManager:didRangeBeacons:inRegion

The `locationManager:didRangeBeacons:inRegion` method is called whenever a beacon (or a number of beacons) change distance from the device. We'll cover ranging beacons more in *Chapter 4, Ranging Beacons – Hunting for Treasure*. For now, it's enough to know that each beacon that's returned in this array has a property called proximity, which returns a `CLProximity` enum value (`CLProximityUnknown`, `CLProximityFar`, `CLProximityNear`, and `CLProximityImmediate`), shown as follows:

```
-(void)locationManager:(CLLocationManager *)manager
   didRangeBeacons:(NSArray *)beacons inRegion:
   (CLBeaconRegion *)region {
      // Do something with the array of beacons.
}
```

## locationManager:didChangeAuthorizationStatus

Finally, there's one more delegate method to cover. Whenever the users grant or deny authorization to use their location, `locationManager:didChangeAuthorizationStatus` is called. This method is passed as a `CLAuthorizationStatus` enum (`kCLAuthorizationStatusNotDetermined`, `kCLAuthorizationStatusRestricted`, `kCLAuthorizationStatusDenied`, and `kCLAuthorizationStatusAuthorized`), shown as follows:

```
-(void)locationManager:(CLLocationManager *)manager
  didChangeAuthorizationStatus:(CLAuthorizationStatus)status {
    // Do something with the array of beacons.
}
```

## Understanding iBeacon permissions

It's important to understand that apps using the Core Location framework are essentially monitoring location, and therefore, they have to ask the user for their permission. The authorization status of a given application is managed by the system and determined by several factors. Applications must be explicitly authorized to use location services by the user, and the current location services must themselves be enabled for the system. A request for user authorization is displayed automatically when your application first attempts to use location services.

Requesting the location can be a fine balancing act. Asking for permission at a point in an app, when your user wouldn't think it was relevant, makes it more likely that they will decline it. It makes more sense to tell the users why you're requesting their location and why it benefits them before requesting it so as not to scare away your more squeamish users.

Building those kinds of information views isn't covered in this book, but to demonstrate the way a user is asked for permission, our app should show an alert like this:

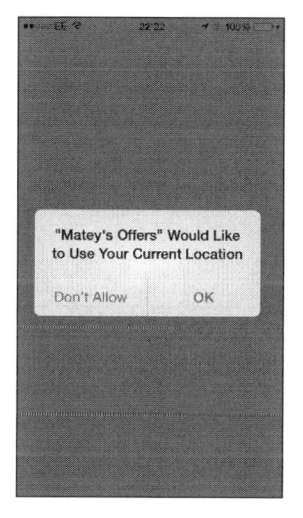

Requesting location permission

If your user taps **Don't Allow**, then the location can't be enabled through the app unless it's deleted and reinstalled. The only way to allow location after denying it is through the settings.

## Location permissions in iOS 8

Since iOS 8.0, additional steps are required to obtain location permissions. In order to request location in iOS 8.0, you must now provide a friendly message in the app's plist by using the `NSLocationAlwaysUsageDescription` key, and also make a call to the `CLLocationManager` class' `requestAlwaysAuthorization` method.

The `NSLocationAlwaysUsageDescription` key describes the reason the app accesses the user's location information. Include this key when your app uses location services in a potentially nonobvious way while running in the foreground or the background.

*Detecting Beacons – Showing an Advert*

There are two types of location permission requests as of iOS 8 as specified by the following plist keys:

- `NSLocationWhenInUseUsageDescription`: This plist key is required when you use the `requestAlwaysAuthorization` method of the `CLLocationManager` class to request authorization for location services. If this key is not present and you call the `requestAlwaysAuthorization` method, the system ignores your request and prevents your app from using location services.

- `NSLocationAlwaysUsageDescription`: This key is required when you use the `requestWhenInUseAuthorization` method of the `CLLocationManager` class to request authorization for location services. If the key is not present when you call the `requestWhenInUseAuthorization` method without including this key, the system ignores your request.

Since iBeacon requires location services in the background, we will only ever use the `NSLocationAlwaysUsageDescription` key with the call to the `CLLocationManager` class' `requestAlwaysAuthorization`.

## Enabling the location after denying it

If a user denies enabling location services, you can follow the given steps to enable the service again on iOS 7:

1. Open the iOS device settings and tap on **Privacy**.
2. Go to the **Location Services** section.
3. Turn location services on for your app by flicking the switch next to your app name.

When your device is running iOS 8, you need to follow these steps:

1. Open the iOS device settings and tap on **Privacy**.
2. Go to your app in the **Settings** menu.
3. Tap on **Privacy**.
4. Tap on **Location Services**.
5. Set the **Allow Location Access** to **Always**.

# Building the tutorial app

To demonstrate the knowledge gained in this chapter, we're going to build an app for our imaginary department store Matey's. Matey's is trialing iBeacons with their app Matey's offers. People with the app get special offers in store as we explained earlier.

For the app, we're going to start a single view application containing two controllers. The first is the default view controller, which will act as our `CLLocationManagerDelegate`, the second is a view controller that will be shown modally and shows the details of the offer relating to the beacon we've come into proximity with.

The final thing to consider is that we'll only show each offer once in a session and we can only show an offer if one isn't showing. Shall we begin?

## Creating the app

Let's start by firing up Xcode and choosing a new single view application just as we did in the previous chapter. Choose these values for the new project:

- **Product Name**: `Matey's Offers`
- **Organization Name**: `Learning iBeacon`
- **Company Identifier**: `com.learning-iBeacon`
- **Class Prefix**: `LI`
- **Devices**: `iPhone`

Your project should now contain your `LIAppDelegate` and `LIViewController` classes. We're not going to touch the app delegate this time round, but we'll need to add some code to the `LIViewController` class since this is where all of our `CLLocationManager` code will be running. For now though, let's leave it to come back to later.

## Adding CLOfferViewController

Our offer view controller will be used as a modal view controller to show the offer relating to the beacon that we come in contact with. Each of our offers is going to be represented with a different background color, a title, and an image to demonstrate the offer.

*Detecting Beacons – Showing an Advert*

Be sure to download the code relating to this chapter and add the three images contained therein to your project by dragging the images from finder into the project navigator:

- `ladiesclothing.jpg`
- `pizza.jpg`
- `sushi.jpg`

Next, we need to create the view controller. Add a new file and be sure to choose the template **Objective-c class** from the **iOS Cocoa Touch** menu. When prompted, name this class `LIOfferViewController` and make it a subclass of `UIViewController`.

# Setting location permission settings

We need to add our permission message to the applications so that when we request permission for the location, our dialog appears:

1. Click on the project file in the project navigator to show the project settings.
2. Click the **Info** tab of the **Matey's Offers** target.
3. Under the **Custom iOS Target Properties** dictionary, add the `NSLocationAlwaysUsageDescription` key with the value. This app needs your location to give you wonderful offers.

# Adding some controls

The offer view controller needs two controls to show the offer the view is representing, an image view and a label. Consider the following steps to add some controls to the view controller:

1. Open the `LIOfferViewController.h` file and add the following properties to the header:

   ```
   @property (nonatomic, strong) UILabel * offerLabel;
   @property (nonatomic, strong) UIImageView * offerImageView;
   ```

2. Now, we need to create them. Open the `LIOfferViewController.m` file and first, let's synthesize the controls. Add the following code just below the `@implementation LIOfferViewController` line:

   ```
   @synthesize offerLabel;
   @synthesize offerImageView;
   ```

3. We've declared the controls; now, we need to actually create them. Within the `viewDidLoad` method, we need to create the label and image view. We don't need to set the actual values or images of our controls. This will be done by `LIViewController` when it encounters a beacon.

4. Create the label by adding the following code below the call to [super viewDidLoad]. This will instantiate the label making it 300 points wide and appear 10 points from the left and top:

   ```
   UILabel * label = [[UILabel alloc]
      initWithFrame:CGRectMake(10, 10, 300, 100)];
   ```

5. Now, we need to set some properties to style the label. We want our label to be center aligned, white in color, and with bold text. We also want it to auto wrap when it's too wide to fit the 300 point width. Add the following code:

   ```
   [label setTextAlignment:NSTextAlignmentCenter];
   [label setTextColor:[UIColor whiteColor]];
   [label setFont:[UIFont boldSystemFontOfSize:22.f]];
   label.numberOfLines = 0; // Allow the label to auto wrap.
   ```

6. Now, we need to add our new label to the view and assign it to our property:

   ```
   [self.view addSubview:label];
   self.offerLabel = label;
   ```

7. Next, we need to create an image. Our image needs a nice border; so to do this, we need to add the QuartzCore framework. Add the QuartzCore framework like we did with CoreLocation in the previous chapter, and come to mention it, we'll need CoreLocation; so, add that too.

8. Once that's done add #import <QuartzCore/QuartzCore.h> to the top of the LIOfferViewController.m file. Now, add the following code to instantiate the image view and add it to our view:

   ```
   UIImageView * imageView = [[UIImageView alloc]
      initWithFrame:CGRectMake(10, 120, 300, 300)];
   [imageView.layer setBorderColor:[[UIColor
      whiteColor] CGColor]];
   [imageView.layer setBorderWidth:2.f];
   imageView.contentMode = UIViewContentModeScaleToFill;
   [self.view addSubview:imageView];
   self.offerImageView = imageView;
   ```

## Setting up our root view controller

Let's jump to LIViewController now and start looking for beacons. We'll start by telling LIViewController that LIOfferViewController exists and also that the view controller should act as a location manager delegate. Consider the following steps:

1. Open LIViewController.h and add an import to the top of the file:

   ```
   #import <CoreLocation/CoreLocation.h>
   #import "LIOfferViewController.h"
   ```

[45]

*Detecting Beacons – Showing an Advert*

2. Now, add the `CLLocationManagerDelegate` protocol to the declaration:

   ```
   @interface LIViewController :
       UIViewController<CLLocationManagerDelegate>
   ```

3. `LIViewController` also needs three things to manage its roll:
   - A reference to the current offer on display so that we know to show only one offer at a time
   - An instance of `CLLocationManager` for monitoring beacons
   - A list of offers seen so that we only show each offer once

4. Let's add these three things to the interface in the `CLViewController.m` file (as they're private instances). Change the `LIViewController` interface to look like this:

   ```
   @interface LIViewController ()
       @property (nonatomic, strong) CLLocationManager *
         locationManager;
       @property (nonatomic, strong) NSMutableDictionary *
         offersSeen;
       @property (nonatomic, strong) LIOfferViewController *
         currentOffer;
   @end
   ```

## Configuring our location manager

Our location manager needs to be configured when the root view controller is first created, and also when the app becomes active. It makes sense therefore that we put this logic into a method. Our reset beacon method needs to do the following things:

- Clear down our list of offers seen
- Request permission to the user's location
- Create a region and set our `LIViewController` instance as the delegate
- Create a beacon region and tell `CLLocationManager` to start ranging beacons

Let's add the code to do this now:

```
-(void)resetBeacons {
// Initialize the location manager.
self.locationManager = [[CLLocationManager alloc] init];
self.locationManager.delegate = self;

// Request permission.
[self.locationManager requestAlwaysAuthorization];
```

```
    // Clear the offers seen.
    self.offersSeen = [[NSMutableDictionary alloc]
      initWithCapacity:3];

    // Create a region.
    NSUUID * regionId = [[NSUUID alloc] initWithUUIDString:
      @"8F0C1DDC-11E5-4A07-8910-425941B072F9"];

    CLBeaconRegion * beaconRegion = [[CLBeaconRegion alloc]
      initWithProximityUUID:regionId identifier:@"Mateys"];

    // Start monitoring and ranging beacons.
    [self.locationManager stopRangingBeaconsInRegion:beaconRegion];
    [self.locationManager startMonitoringForRegion:beaconRegion];
    [self.locationManager startRangingBeaconsInRegion:beaconRegion];
}
```

Now, add the two calls to the reset beacon to ensure that the location manager is reset when the app is first started and then every time the app becomes active.

Let's add this code now by changing the `viewDidLoad` method and adding the `applicationDidBecomeActive` method:

```
-(void)viewDidLoad {
    [super viewDidLoad];
    [self resetBeacons];
}

- (void)applicationDidBecomeActive:(UIApplication *)application
{
    [self resetBeacons];
}
```

## Wiring up CLLocationManagerDelegate

Now, we need to wire up the delegate methods of the `CLLocationManagerDelegate` protocol so that `CLViewController` can show the offer view when the beacons come into proximity.

The first thing we need to do is to set the background color of the view to show whether or not our app has been authorized to use the device location. If the authorization has not yet been determined, we'll use orange. If the app has been authorized, we'll use green. Finally, if the app has been denied, we'll use red.

We'll be using the `locationManager:didChangeAuthorizationStatus` delegate method to do this.

## Detecting Beacons – Showing an Advert

Let's add the code now:

```
-(void)locationManager:(CLLocationManager *)manager
  didChangeAuthorizationStatus:(CLAuthorizationStatus)
  status {
    switch (status) {
      case kCLAuthorizationStatusNotDetermined:
      {
          // Set a lovely orange background
          [self.view setBackgroundColor:[UIColor
            colorWithRed:255.f/255.f green:147.f/255.f
            blue:61.f/255.f alpha:1.f]];
          break;
      }
      case kCLAuthorizationStatusAuthorized:
      {
          // Set a lovely green background.
          [self.view setBackgroundColor:[UIColor
            colorWithRed:99.f/255.f green:185.f/255.f
            blue:89.f/255.f alpha:1.f]];
          break;
      }
      default:
      {
          // Set a dark red background.
          [self.view setBackgroundColor:[UIColor
            colorWithRed:188.f/255.f green:88.f/255.f
            blue:88.f/255.f alpha:1.f]];
          break;
      }
    }
}
```

The next thing we need to do is to save the battery life by stopping and starting the ranging of beacons when we're within the region (except for when the app first starts). We do this by calling the `startRangingBeaconsInRegion` method with the `locationManager:didEnterRegion` delegate method and calling the `stopRangingBeaconsInRegion` method within the `locationManager:didExitRegion` delegate method.

Add the following code to do what we've just described:

```
-(void)locationManager:(CLLocationManager *)manager
  didEnterRegion:(CLRegion *)region {
    [self.locationManager
      startRangingBeaconsInRegion:(CLBeaconRegion*)region];
```

```
}
-(void)locationManager:(CLLocationManager *)manager
    didExitRegion:(CLRegion *)region {
      [self.locationManager
        stopRangingBeaconsInRegion:(CLBeaconRegion*)region];
}
```

## Showing the advert

To actually show the advert, we need to capture when a beacon is ranged by adding the `locationManager:didRangeBeacons:inRegion` delegate method to `LIViewController`. This method will be called every time the distance changes from an already discovered beacon in our region or when a new beacon is found for the region.

The implementation is quite long so I'm going to explain each part of the method as we write it.

Start by creating the method implementation as follows:

```
-(void)locationManager:(CLLocationManager *)manager
    didRangeBeacons:(NSArray *)beacons inRegion:
    (CLBeaconRegion *)region {

}
```

We only want to show an offer associated with the beacon if we've not seen it before and there isn't a current offer being shown. We do this by checking the `currentOffer` property. If this property isn't nil, it means an offer is already being displayed and so, we need to return from the method.

The `locationManager:didRangeBeacons:inRegion` method gets called by the location manager and gets passed to the region instance and an array of beacons that are currently in range. We only want to see each advert once in a session and so need to loop through each of the beacons to determine if we've seen it before.

Let's add a `for` loop to iterate through the beacons and in the beacon looping do an initial check to see if there's an offer already showing:

```
for (CLBeacon * beacon in beacons) {
    if (self.currentOffer) return;
}
```

# Detecting Beacons – Showing an Advert

Our `offersSeen` property is `NSMutableDictionary` containing all the beacons (and subsequently offers) that we've already seen. The key consists of the major and minor values of the beacon in the format {major|minor}.

Let's create a string using the major and minor values and check whether this string exists in our `offersSeen` property by adding the following code to the loop:

```
NSString * majorMinorValue = [NSString stringWithFormat:
  @"%@|%@", beacon.major, beacon.minor];
if ([self.offersSeen objectForKey:majorMinorValue]) continue;
```

If `offersSeen` contains the key, then we continue looping.

If the offer hasn't been seen, then we need to add it to the offers that are seen, before presenting the offer.

Let's start by adding the key to our offers that are seen in the dictionary and then preparing an instance of `LIOfferViewController`:

```
[self.offersSeen setObject:[NSNumber numberWithBool:YES]
   forKey:majorMinorValue];
LIOfferViewController * offerVc = [[LIOfferViewController alloc]
   init];
offerVc.modalPresentationStyle = UIModalPresentationFullScreen;
```

Now, we're going prepare some variables to configure the offer view controller. Food offers show with a blue background while clothing offers show with a red background.

We use the major value of the beacon to determine the color and then find out the image and label based on the minor value:

```
UIColor * backgroundColor;
NSString * labelValue;
UIImage * productImage;

// Major value 1 is food, 2 is clothing.
if ([beacon.major intValue] == 1) {

    // Blue signifies food.
    backgroundColor = [UIColor colorWithRed:89.f/255.f
       green:159.f/255.f blue:208.f/255.f alpha:1.f];

    if ([beacon.minor intValue] == 1) {
        labelValue = @"30% off sushi at the Japanese Kitchen.";
        productImage = [UIImage imageNamed:@"sushi.jpg"];
    }
```

```
    else {
        labelValue = @"Buy one get one free at
          Tucci's Pizza.";
        productImage = [UIImage imageNamed:@"pizza.jpg"];
    }
}
else {
    // Red signifies clothing.
    backgroundColor = [UIColor colorWithRed:188.f/255.f
      green:88.f/255.f blue:88.f/255.f alpha:1.f];
    labelValue = @"50% off all ladies clothing.";
    productImage = [UIImage imageNamed:@"ladiesclothing.jpg"];
}
```

Finally, we need to set these values on the view controller and present it modally. We also need to set our `currentOffer` property to be the view controller so that we don't show more than one color at the same time:

```
[offerVc.view setBackgroundColor:backgroundColor];
[offerVc.offerLabel setText:labelValue];
[offerVc.offerImageView setImage:productImage];
[self presentViewController:offerVc animated:YES
  completion:nil];
self.currentOffer = offerVc;
```

## Dismissing the offer

Since `LIOfferViewController` is a modal view, we're going to need a dismiss button; however, we also need some way of telling it to our root view controller (`LIViewController`). Consider the following steps:

1. Add the following code to the `LIViewController.h` interface to declare a public method:

    ```
    -(void)offerDismissed;
    ```

2. Now, add the implementation to `LIViewController.h`. This method simply clears the `currentOffer` property as the actual dismiss is handled by the offer view controller:

    ```
    -(void)offerDismissed {
        self.currentOffer = nil;
    }
    ```

3. Now, let's jump back to `LIOfferViewController`. Add the following code to the end of the `viewDidLoad` method of `LIOfferViewController` to create a dismiss button:

   ```
   UIButton * dismissButton = [[UIButton alloc]
     initWithFrame:CGRectMake(60.f, 440.f, 200.f, 44.f)];
   [self.view addSubview:dismissButton];
   [dismissButton setTitle:@"Dismiss"
     forState:UIControlStateNormal];
   [dismissButton setTitleColor:[UIColor whiteColor]
     forState:UIControlStateNormal];
   [dismissButton addTarget:self
     action:@selector(dismissTapped:)
     forControlEvents:UIControlEventTouchUpInside];
   ```

   As you can see, the touch up event calls `@selector(dismissTapped:)`, which doesn't exist yet. We can get a handle of `LIViewController` through the app delegate (which is an instance of `LIAppDelegate`). In order to use this, we need to import it and `LIViewController`.

4. Add the following imports to the top of `LIOfferViewController.m`:

   ```
   #import "LIViewController.h"
   #import "LIAppDelegate.h"
   ```

5. Finally, let's complete the tutorial by adding the `dismissTapped` method:

   ```
   -(void)dismissTapped:(UIButton*)sender {
       [self dismissViewControllerAnimated:YES completion:^{
           LIAppDelegate * delegate =
             (LIAppDelegate*)[UIApplication
             sharedApplication].delegate;
           LIViewController * rootVc =
             (LIViewController*)delegate.
             window.rootViewController;
           [rootVc offerDismissed];
       }];
   }
   ```

Now, let's run our app. You should be presented with the location permission request as shown in the *Requesting location permission* figure, from the *Understanding iBeacon permissions* section. Tap on OK and then fire up the companion app. Play around with the **Chapter 2** beacon configurations by turning them on and off. What you should see is something like the following figure:

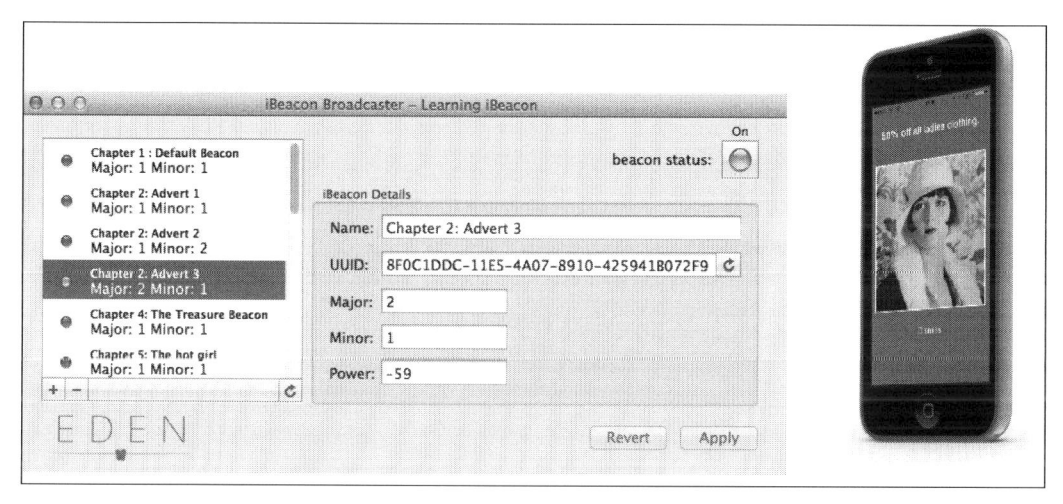

*Our app working with the companion OS X app*

Remember that your app should only show one offer at a time and your beacon should only show each offer once per session.

# Summary

Well done on completing your first real iBeacon powered app, which actually differentiates between beacons. In this chapter, we covered the real usage of UUID, major, and minor values. We also got introduced to the Core Location framework including the `CLLocationManager` class and its important delegate methods. We introduced the `CLRegion` class and discussed the permissions required when using `CLLocationManager`.

Finally, we put this all together with offers from our Matey's store.

In the next chapter, we're going to broadcast offers using our iOS device as an iBeacon transmitter.

# 3
# Broadcasting Advertisements – Sending Offers

In the previous chapter, we used the companion beacon app and learned how to react when we come into the range of beacons. We built the Matey's offers app to show offers around the store. In this chapter, we're going to look at the other side and we're going to become Matey's by actually using our iOS device to broadcast offers.

## Introducing the Core Bluetooth framework

Let's start with a new framework that makes broadcasting possible: Core Bluetooth. In this chapter, we'll still be using the Core Location framework but only to configure our transmitter. This chapter is all about the technology behind beacons.

The Core Bluetooth framework provides the classes needed for your iOS and Mac apps to communicate with the Bluetooth's low energy wireless technology.

Core Bluetooth has been available since iOS 6.0 and is intended solely for the implementation of centrals and peripherals.

## Understanding centrals and peripherals

Before we understand how to broadcast as a beacon, it's worth understanding what centrals and peripherals are. If you think about peripherals as devices that have data and centrals as devices that want data, this makes the concept much easier to understand.

Peripherals are things such as thermostats, heart monitors, blood pressure monitors, proximity sensors, lamps, lights, and LED bulbs. They are devices that collect data or receive commands and they advertise their data such as iBeacons.

Centrals are things such as iPhones, iPads, and home automation servers that collate or act on this data.

Consider the following figure: if the peripheral in question is a thermostat, it will broadcast its presence and the temperature together. It wouldn't really need to receive data unless there were some configuration options available via **Bluetooth low energy** (**Bluetooth LE**).

Now, consider that the beacon might be an LED light with multicolor capability. The peripheral here has two roles: to broadcast its current color and also allow a central to transmit a command back so that the user can set the color of his/her room as per his/her mood using an iPhone app.

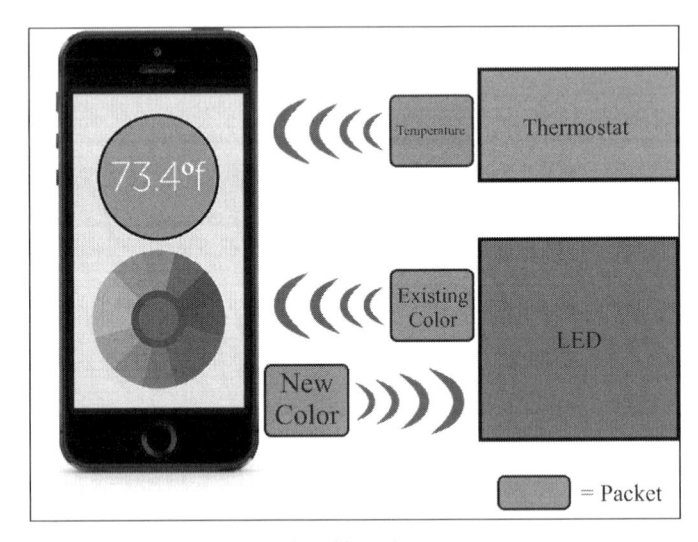

Peripheral broadcasting

# The Core Bluetooth framework, centrals, and peripherals

The Core Bluetooth framework provides an abstract implementation of the central and peripheral requirements. Let's look at each class in a little more detail.

## The CBCentral class

The `CBCentral` class represents a central in a BLE implementation that is currently connected to you while implementing the peripheral role using the `CBPeripheralManager` class. The central used to represent classes that are currently connected when your app is performing the peripheral role and you want to update the central with new values.

## The CBPeripheral class

The `CBPeripheral` class represents the remote peripherals that your app has discovered while advertising and can connect to (or are already connected to).

The `CBPeripheral` class lets your app interact with peripherals that you discover using the `CBCentralManager` class. The `CBPeripheral` class lets you query, discover characteristics, discover services, and monitor connections to the peripherals.

## The CBPeripheralManager class

Instances of the `CBPeripheralManager` class are used to manage and publish peripheral data of the capabilities of your device. In the simplest of terms, it allows you to broadcast as a BLE peripheral (among other things). As you can probably guess, this is the class we're most interested in for this chapter.

> We'll also be using a `CLBeaconRegion` instance to collate a dictionary of values to broadcast as an iBeacon with this class.

The `CBPeripheralManagerDelegate` protocol is required to make the peripheral manager useful to us, and the most important thing to remember is that `CBPeripheralManager` can't really do anything if the device doesn't have BLE capability or the Bluetooth adapter isn't powered on yet. To determine the state of the Bluetooth adapter, you need to use the `peripheralManagerDidUpdateState:` protocol method, which we'll be doing in our tutorial.

Our `CBPeripheralManager` class acts as a beacon using the `startAdvertising` method, which takes a dictionary of values to broadcast. It gets this dictionary from `CLBeaconRegion`.

# Obtaining broadcast values from CLBeaconRegion

In order to use the `startAdvertising` method of the `CBPeripheralManage` class, we need to know what we're broadcasting. We do this by calling the `peripheralDataWithMeasuredPower:` method of `CLBeaconRegion`. The resulting `NSMutableDictionary` class can be used with the `startAdvertising` method of the `CBPeripheralManage` class.

## Measured power (TXPower)

Back in *Chapter 1, Welcome to iBeacon*, we discussed RSSI and measured power to adjust the power of the transmission so that the distance could be better understood. We'll put this principle into effect during the tutorial by using the measured power of -63 dBm, which should give the correct RSSI value at distance of 1 meter. This might not be completely accurate as it's hardware-dependent, but it should be pretty close.

## Let's get started

To build our app, we need two devices. One device should be running the tutorial from *Chapter 2, Detecting Beacons – Showing an Advert* as a receiver and the second device is what we'll be using to build our transmission app.

We'll be using storyboards to build a universal app, which will broadcast each of the offers from *Chapter 2, Detecting Beacons – Showing an Advert*. We'll be broadcasting the values using a `CBPeripheralManager` object and the project will be a single view application.

Let's get started by creating a universal single view application.

Fire up Xcode and create a new project. When prompted, choose **Single View Application** from the **iOS | Application** menu.

When choosing options for the project, enter the following details as shown:

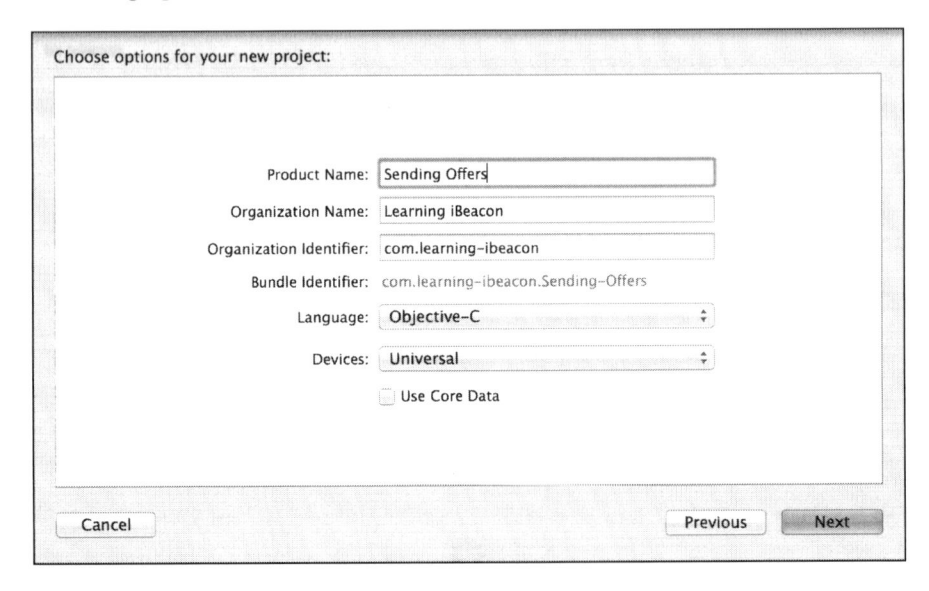

Choose where you want to save your project. You should now have `LIAppDelegate`, `LIViewController`, `Main_iPhone.storyboard`, and `Main_iPad.storyboard`.

We'll only be working with the storyboards and `LIViewController`. If you want to use any of the images in the **Download** folder to embellish, then feel free.

## Adding frameworks

We'll be using Core Bluetooth and Core Location in this project. Click on the project in the project navigator (⌘1) and under the **General** tab, click on the **+** button under **Linked Frameworks and Libraries**. Add the Core Location and Core Bluetooth frameworks.

## Setting up our controls

Now, we need to set up our view controls to allow the user to change the broadcasting advert. Jump on to the `LIViewController.h` file, where we'll be presenting the following things:

- A label to give some context to the `CBPeripheralManager` status
- A switch to send the sushi offer from *Chapter 2, Detecting Beacons – Showing an Advert*
- Another switch for the pizza offer
- One final switch for the ladies' clothing offer

Let's start by configuring these properties. Remember that we're using storyboards, so these properties need to be `IBOutlet`. Add the following code to the header file:

```
@property (nonatomic, weak) IBOutlet UILabel * offerLabel;
@property (nonatomic, weak) IBOutlet UISwitch * sushiSwitch;
@property (nonatomic, weak) IBOutlet UISwitch * pizzaSwitch;
@property (nonatomic, weak) IBOutlet UISwitch * clothingSwitch;
```

We also need to define an action for when the switches change state. Let's add that too:

```
- (IBAction)offerSwitchValueChanged:(id)sender;
```

## Creating our views

Let's open `Main_iPhone.storyboard` and create our view. Since we chose a single view application from the options when we created the project, Xcode should have already wired up a view to `LIViewController`. Consider the following steps to create views:

1. Drag three switches and three labels for those switches onto the view. Set the text for those labels to represent what the switches do. Ensure that you disable the switches inside the attributes selector. We'll enable the switches in the code when `BLPeripheralManager` is available. The labels can represent the switches with text as follows:
    - **30% off sushi**
    - **Buy one get one free pizza**
    - **50% off ladies clothing**

2. Add `UILabel` to the bottom of the view to represent the `BLPeripheralManager` status. If you're feeling artistic, then you can add images too. I've created a Matey's logo, which is available in the code bundle for this chapter. Your view should now look something like the following screenshot:

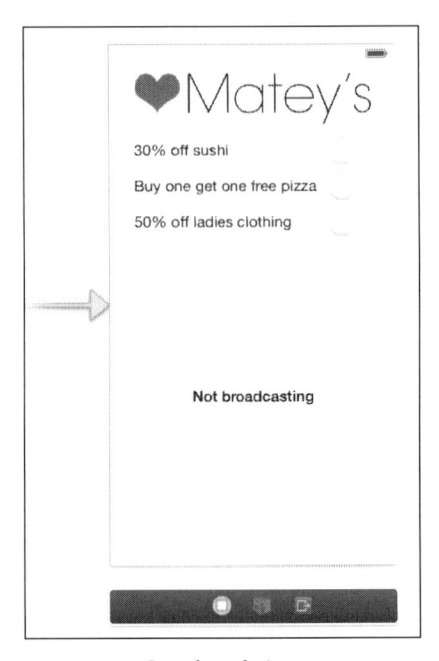

Storyboard view

Go ahead and do the same for `Main_iPad.storyboard` too.

## Wiring up the storyboard

Next, we need to wire the storyboard controls to our view controller. We can do this using the assistant editor, which can be shown by pressing *alt + command + enter*. Follow these steps to wire up the storyboard:

1. Using the assistant editor, ensure the storyboard is open on the left pane and `LIViewController.h` on the right pane. Click on the switch you want to bind on the left pane and drag it to the properties in the right pane while holding the *control* key as shown in following figure.

2. Do this for all the three switches and also for the offer label.

3. Finally, bind the actions of all the three switches to `IBAction` `offerSwitchValueChanged`.

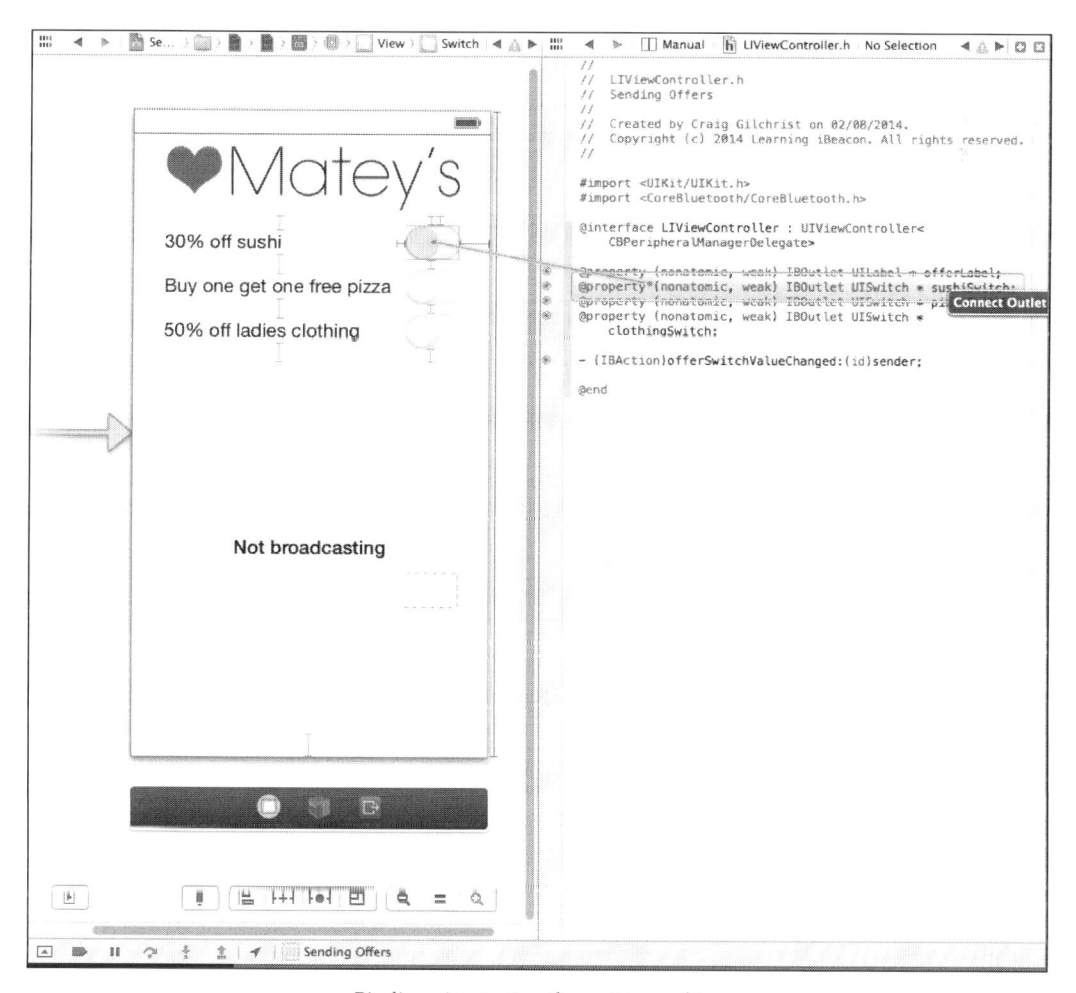

Binding views using the assistant editor

## Setting up our view controller

Now that we've wired up the entire user interface, it's time to configure our view controller. Let's start by adding our `CoreBluetooth` and `CoreLocation` library imports to the `LIViewController.h` file.

We also need to make our view controller `CBPeripheralManagerDelegate`. Add the following code to your `LIViewController.h` file:

```
#import <CoreBluetooth/CoreBluetooth.h>
#import <CoreLocation/CoreLocation.h>

@interface LIViewController :
    UIViewController<CBPeripheralManagerDelegate>
```

Now, jump over to the `LIViewController.m` file. We're going to need the unique ID for the region. Add this as `static` before the internal interface declaration, right at the top:

```
static NSString * uuid = @"8F0C1DDC-11E5-4A07-8910-425941B072F9";
```

We're going to need some private properties to keep a track of our peripheral manager and the peripheral broadcast dictionary. Let's overwrite the private interface with our own implementation:

```
@interface LIViewController ()
@property (nonatomic, strong) CBPeripheralManager *
   peripheralManager;
@property (nonatomic, strong) NSDictionary * sushiPeripheralData;
@property (nonatomic, strong) NSDictionary * pizzaPeripheralData;
@property (nonatomic, strong) NSDictionary *
   clothingPeripheralData;
@end
```

We'll need a new region to create the peripheral data. In fact, we'll need one for each dictionary. Let's set these up in the `ViewDidLoad` method, as shown:

```
// Prepare the uuid.
NSUUID * uid = [[NSUUID alloc] initWithUUIDString:uuid];
CLBeaconRegion * sushiRegion = [[CLBeaconRegion alloc]
   initWithProximityUUID:uid major:1 minor:1 identifier:
   @"Matey's Sushi"];
CLBeaconRegion * pizzaRegion = [[CLBeaconRegion alloc]
   initWithProximityUUID:uid major:1 minor:2 identifier:
   @"Matey's Pizza"];
CLBeaconRegion * clothingRegion = [[CLBeaconRegion alloc]
   initWithProximityUUID:uid major:2 minor:1 identifier:
   @"Matey's Clothing"];
```

Now that we've got our regions, let's set up peripheral data using them. Remember that to do this, we need a measured power value, as shown:

```
NSNumber * power = [NSNumber numberWithInt:-63];

// Use the beacon region to create the peripheral data.
self.sushiPeripheralData = [[sushiRegion
  peripheralDataWithMeasuredPower:power] copy];
self.pizzaPeripheralData = [[pizzaRegion
  peripheralDataWithMeasuredPower:power] copy];
self.clothingPeripheralData = [[clothingRegion
  peripheralDataWithMeasuredPower:power] copy];
```

Finally, we need to instantiate our peripheral manager. To do this, we need a dispatch queue for broadcasting and to set the delegate as our view controller, shown as follows:

```
dispatch_queue_t queue =
  dispatch_get_global_queue(DISPATCH_QUEUE_PRIORITY_DEFAULT, 0);
self.peripheralManager = [[CBPeripheralManager alloc]
  initWithDelegate:self queue:queue];
```

We need to wire up the delegate method `peripheralManagerDidUpdateState` so that we can enable the switches when the peripheral manager is available. Let's add this code now:

```
-(void)peripheralManagerDidUpdateState:(CBPeripheralManager
  *)peripheral {
    if (peripheral.state == CBPeripheralManagerStatePoweredOn) {
        // Enable the buttons.
        [self.pizzaSwitch setEnabled:YES];
        [self.sushiSwitch setEnabled:YES];
        [self.clothingSwitch setEnabled:YES];
    }
    else {
        [self.offerLabel setText:@"Bluetooth not enabled"];
    }
}
```

## Adding our switch logic

The final thing to do is to start advertising when switches are flicked. Since all switches utilize the `offerSwitchValueChanged` method, we need to implement it:

```
- (IBAction)offerSwitchValueChanged:(id)sender {
}
```

## Broadcasting Advertisements – Sending Offers

We should ever broadcast only one item at a time from our app, and so the first thing to do in this method is to stop advertising if we already are. Add the call to stop the peripheral manager from broadcasting to the method:

```
[self.peripheralManager stopAdvertising];
```

We need to understand which switch has called the selector and turn the rest of the switches off. We also need to know what advertising data to send and also what status message to show. Add this code now:

```
// Cast the sender to a switch.
    UISwitch * senderSwitch = (UISwitch*)sender;

    NSDictionary * advertData;
    NSString * advertString;

    if (senderSwitch == self.sushiSwitch) {
        [self.pizzaSwitch setOn:NO animated:YES];
        [self.clothingSwitch setOn:NO animated:YES];
        advertData = self.sushiPeripheralData;
        advertString = @"Offering 30% off sushi";
    }

    if (senderSwitch == self.pizzaSwitch) {
        [self.sushiSwitch setOn:NO animated:YES];
        [self.clothingSwitch setOn:NO animated:YES];
        advertData = self.pizzaPeripheralData;
        advertString = @"Offering Buy one get one free on all
           pizza";
    }

    if (senderSwitch == self.clothingSwitch) {
        [self.pizzaSwitch setOn:NO animated:YES];
        [self.sushiSwitch setOn:NO animated:YES];
        advertData = self.clothingPeripheralData;
        advertString = @"Offering 50% off ladies clothing";
    }
```

Finally, we need to know whether the switch is on or off in order to know whether we need to start advertising the data or not. Let's do this:

```
if (senderSwitch.isOn) {
[self.peripheralManager startAdvertising:advertData];
    [self.offerLabel setText:advertString];
}
else {
    [self.offerLabel setText:@"Not Broadcasting"];
}
```

Et voilà—we're done! Run the app from *Chapter 2, Detecting Beacons – Showing an Advert,* and run the app that we created in this chapter on another device. Turn on each switch in turn to see the ads appear, and dismiss the ad before flicking the next switch on your broadcasting device.

# Summary

We've covered quite a lot for such a short chapter. You learned about the Core Bluetooth framework and a very small subset of the features contained within. I'd recommend delving deeper into this framework using off the shelf hardware There's an excellent article on Ray Wenderlich's website about using an iPhone to interact with the Polar Bluetooth heart rate monitor, which you can find at `http://bit.ly/hr-monitor`.

In the next chapter, we're going to cover determining distance to build a treasure hunt app. We're going to make it exciting by making the app talk as we get closer to the treasure. So, what are ye waiting for me hearties? Let's go!

# 4
# Ranging Beacons – Hunting for Treasure

In the previous chapter, we covered functionality, which is triggered when we come into the range of a beacon. In this chapter, we will range beacons in a pirate-inspired treasure hunt.

We won't cover lots of new features in this chapter; instead, we will focus on honing our existing knowledge and add just one or two more new methods of the `CLLocationManager` class.

In this chapter, we'll cover the following topics:

- Using the `CLLocationManager` class to range beacons
- Detecting the range using the `CLLocationManager didRangeBeacons:inRegion` delegate method of `CLLocationManagerDelegate`

## There be treasure nearby

We will build a treasure-hunting app in this chapter. Ideally, you'll have two compatible iOS devices so that one can be the treasure and another can be the hunter. Don't worry if you have only one iOS device; the companion app can act as the treasure, and your iOS device can be the treasure.

Our app will perform both features using modal view controllers. The main view of the app will simply allow the user to choose whether the device is the treasure or the hunter. Once the user makes his or her choice, the app will open a dedicated view controller with a single role to hunt or to be hunted.

We'll call our treasure view controller `LITreasureViewController` and our hunter view controller `LIHunterViewController`.

When our app runs in treasure mode, it will simply operate as a beacon, much like we did in *Chapter 3, Broadcasting Advertisements – Sending Offers*, when we sent Matey's offers from our iOS device. The app gets more interesting when it is running in hunter mode.

In hunter mode, the app will range the beacons and show the distance on an illustrated map, as seen in the next figure. We'll use the determined distance.

# Understanding distance

When we range beacons using the `locationManager:didRangeBeacons:inRegion` method of `CLLocationManager`, we're given a collection of beacons (`CLBeacon`). In order to understand the distance of the beacon from our device, the `CLBeacon` class gives us two properties:

- `proximity`: The `proximity` property gives you the distance from the device using the `CLProximity` enum, giving one of four values `CLProximityUnknown`, `CLProximityFar`, `CLProximityNear`, and `CLProximityImmediate`.
- `accuracy`: The `accuracy` property gives you the distance from the device as a double value, which is the distance measured in meters. If the distance cannot be determined, the value is returned as negative.

The `CLProximity` enum values represent the approximate distance from the device in four bands and are great to determine when to perform an action.

Imagine you're building an app for a museum. Your app tells users about the individual cabinets within different exhibits as visitors walk through. If your visitor enters an exhibition of Dutch art, and you start playing a video about a Rembrandt painting situated on the other side of the room, you'll be left with a very confused user.

In this instance, you only want to trigger this video when the beacon reports a proximity value of `CLProximityImmediate`.

For most use cases, the proximity property is enough. In circumstances where you're trying to plot a user's position on an internal map accurately, you're most likely to use the accuracy value to triangulate the user's position using multiple beacons.

The upcoming figure represents the approximate distance of the `CLProximity` enum values:

- `CLProximityUnknown`: This represents a distance greater than 30 meters. This is used when a more accurate range cannot be determined.
- `CLProximityFar`: This means that the beacon is still quite far away and represents a distance between 2 to 30 meters.
- `CLProximityNear`: This means that the beacon is reasonably close to the user at a distance between half a meter and 2 meters.
- `CLProximityImmediate`: This means that the beacon is within half a meter; you should be able to touch the beacon.

CLProximity enum values

## Our application

Our app operates in two modes, as shown in the following figure. Both the treasure and hunter modes have independent view controllers to encapsulate their functionality. Our root view controller (`LIViewController`) simply allows us to choose the mode we want to run.

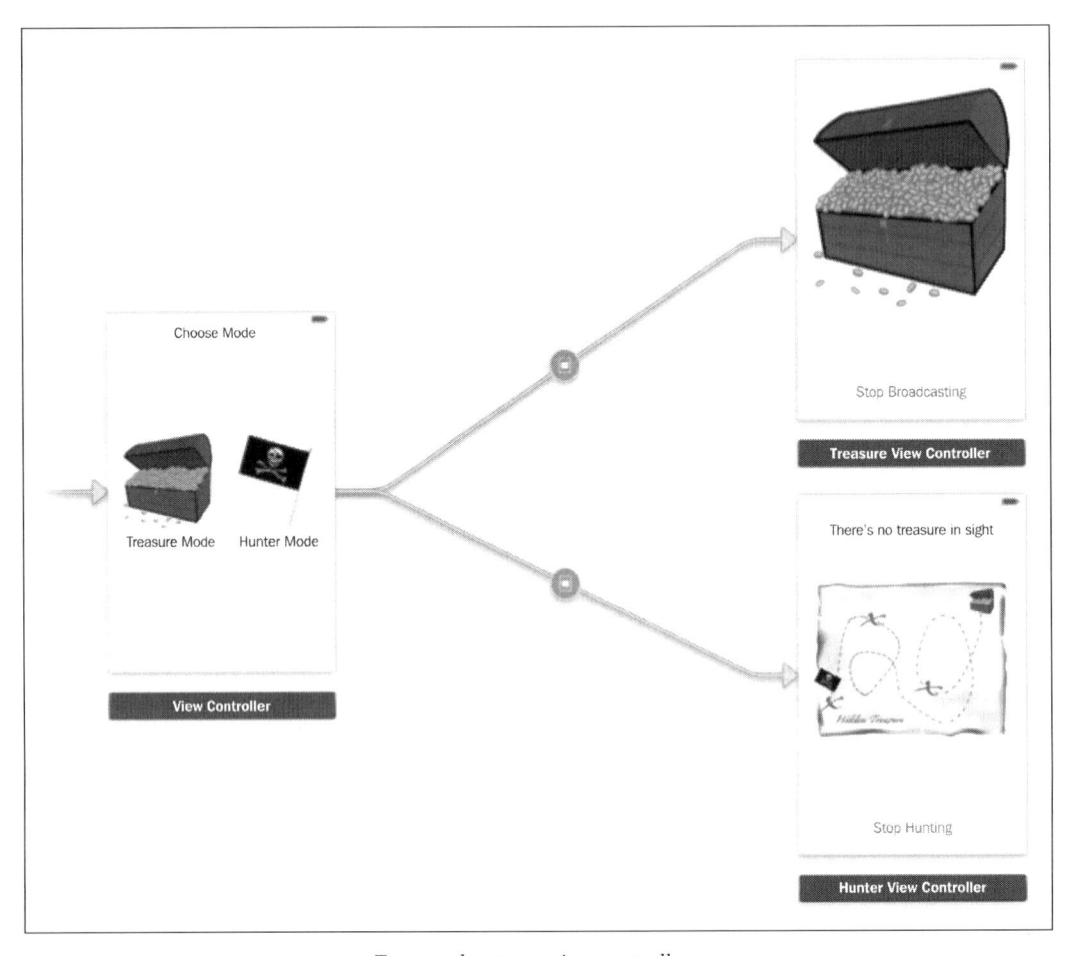

Treasure hunt app view controllers

If you don't have two iOS devices at hand, don't worry; we can use the companion app to broadcast as our treasure beacon, as shown in the following figure. Unfortunately, you can't perform Bluetooth interactions in the simulator. So, unless you have two devices, you'll only be able to test the hunter.

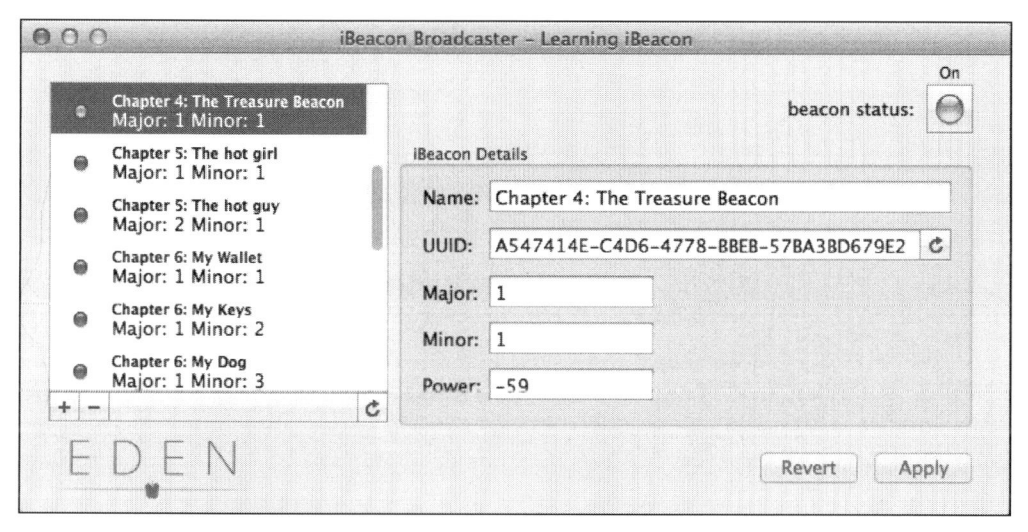

Using the companion app as the treasure

# Getting started with building our app

Consider the following steps to build our app:

1. Fire up Xcode and create a new project. Choose **Single View Application** from the list of templates, and when prompted, use the following values for the new project:
    - **Product Name**: TreasureHunt
    - **Organization Name**: Learning iBeacon
    - **Company Identifier**: com.learning-ibeacon
    - **Class Prefix**: LI
    - **Devices**: Universal

2. We'll need the Core Bluetooth and Core Location frameworks, so go ahead and add them to the project too. If you need help with this, refer to *Chapter 3, Broadcasting Advertisements – Sending Offers*.

# Drawing our initial views

We'll be using storyboards this time round to create our views. We'll write each controller separately, but to get us started, we'll create stubs for these controllers so that we can set up our storyboards. Execute the following steps:

1. Start by creating two new Objective-C classes and subclass them from `UIViewController`. Call these classes `LITreasureViewController` and `LIHunterViewController`.

2. Open the `Main_iPhone.storyboard` file. You'll see that the Xcode template has already created a view for `LIViewController`. We will drop view controllers for each of our modal view controllers.

3. Drag two new view controllers onto the storyboard from **Object Library** (^⌥⌘3).

4. Select the first view controller you added and open **Identity Inspector** (⌥⌘3). Under the custom class, set the value to `LITreasureViewController`. We'll need a way to create an instance of this view controller and view in code, so set the **Storyboard ID** value to `TreasureViewController`.

5. Follow the previous steps for the hunter view, using the following values:
   - **Class**: `LIHunterViewController`
   - **Storyboard ID**: `HunterViewController`

6. Now, let's define how these views get presented using segues. Hold down the *control* key, click, and drag from our root view controller to our treasure view controller. In the resulting segue dialog, choose **modal** as the type, as shown in the following figure. Do the same for the treasure view controller:

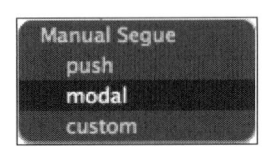

Modal segue options

> Don't forget to do the same for the iPad views over in the `Main_iPhone.storyboard` file. We wouldn't want your iPad app to be missed out.

Let's start coding each of our view controllers now. We can wire up the views as we go.

# Adding frameworks and project settings

We'll need the following frameworks. Add them now:

- CoreLocation
- CoreBluetooth
- QuartzCore

Next, we need to ensure that when our app has the plist setting, ask for location permission to enable it. Add the NSLocationAlwaysDescription key to the **Info** tab of the project settings. Set the value to This app needs your location so that we can find some treasure in your project settings, as shown in the following figure:

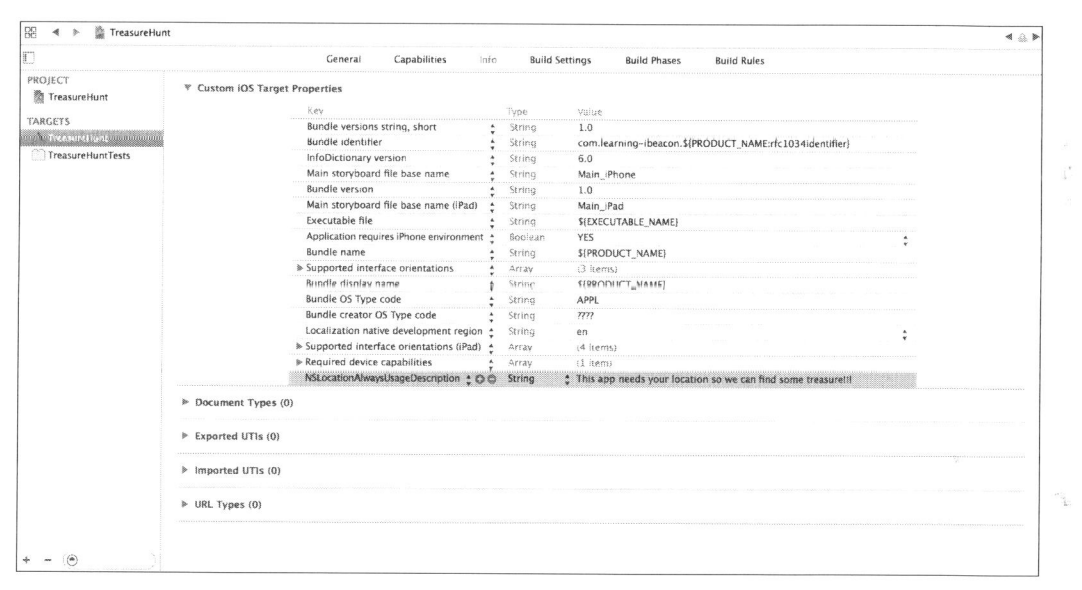

Adding location service description settings

# Adding images

In the available source code, there are six images that we'll need for this app.

Using the downloaded resources, locate the images folder and pull the following files into your application. Ensure you check the **Copy items into destination group's folders (if needed)** option:

- Flat.png. This image is a pirate flag to represent your pirate party on the hunt for treasure

[73]

- `Treasure-Map-1.png`: This image is a treasure map showing you very far away from the treasure (`CLProximityUnknown`)
- `Treasure-Map-2.png`: This image is a treasure map showing you far away from the treasure (`CLProximityFar`)
- `Treasure-Map-3.png`: This image is a treasure map showing you near to the treasure (`CLProximityNear`)
- `Treasure-Map-4.png`: This image is a treasure map showing you in immediate proximity to the treasure (`CLProximityImmediate`)
- `Treasure.png`: This image is a lovely treasure chest filled with treasure

# Building the root view controller

Our root view controller should simply have two buttons to present one of the two functional view controllers modally. There's very little functionality in this controller, so let's just pop it in immediately:

1. Open up the `LIViewController.m` file and create the two IBAction methods that will instantiate a new view controller using the current storyboard and the identifier values that we set earlier before presenting the newly created view controller:

    ```
    - (IBAction)chooseTreasure:(id)sender {
        UIViewController * vc = [self.storyboard
            instantiateViewControllerWithIdentifier:
            @"TreasureViewController"];

        [self presentViewController:vc animated:YES completion:nil];
    }

    - (IBAction)chooseHunter:(id)sender {
        UIViewController * vc = [self.storyboard
            instantiateViewControllerWithIdentifier:
            @"HunterViewController"];

        [self presentViewController:vc animated:YES completion:nil];
    }
    ```

2. Jump back over to the iPhone storyboard file and add some instruction labels and two buttons from **Object Library** (^⌥⌘3). Set the button images to `Treasure.png` and `Flag.png` and lay out your view so that it looks like the following figure. Finally, use the *control* key and drag the view controller buttons to their associated `IBAction` using **Assistant Editor** (⌥⌘↩).

3. Don't forget the iPad storyboard too!

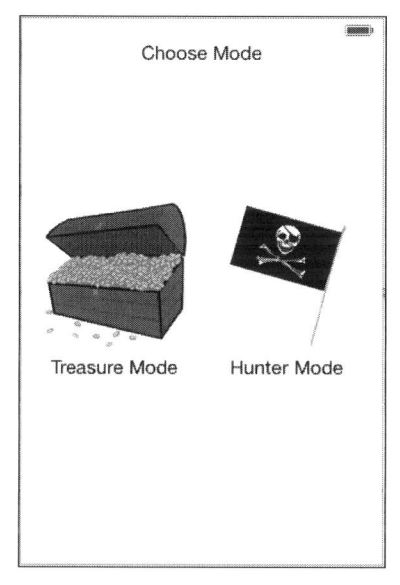

Our root view controller view

## Building the treasure view controller

Our treasure view controller has a simpler UI, but it has a lot more going on behind the scenes.

`LITreasureViewController` will provide the functionality to broadcast a beacon profile using `CBPeripheralManager`, just like what was described in *Chapter 2, Detecting Beacons – Showing an Advert*. This time, we'll need to be neater in our implementation because we need to clean up and stop broadcasting when the app enters the background or the modal view is dismissed.

We will also dismiss this view controller if the iOS device isn't compatible with BLE. We'll do this with an alert message.

The first thing we need to do is declare our view controller as `CBPeripheralManagerDelegate` and `UIAlertViewDelegate`.

1. Open up the `LITreasureViewController.h` file, import the frameworks, and set the delegate declarations as follows:

    ```
    #import <UIKit/UIKit.h>
    #import <CoreBluetooth/CoreBluetooth.h>
    #import <CoreLocation/CoreLocation.h>
    ```

## Ranging Beacons – Hunting for Treasure

```
@interface LITreasureViewController :
  UIViewController<CBPeripheralManagerDelegate,
  UIAlertViewDelegate>
@end
```

2. Now, jump over to the `LITreasureViewController.m` file and declare a `CBPeripheralManager` property in the private interface declaration, as shown in the following code:

```
@interface LITreasureViewController ()
@property (nonatomic, strong) CBPeripheralManager *
  peripheralManager;
@end
```

3. We need a way to dismiss the view controller and stop broadcasting as a beacon. Add the following method:

```
- (IBAction)stopBroadcasting:(id)sender {
    [self.peripheralManager stopAdvertising];
    [self dismissViewControllerAnimated:YES completion:nil];
}
```

As discussed in *Chapter 3, Broadcasting Advertisements – Sending Offers*, we need to wait until `CBPeripheral` is powered up before we can use it, so the responsibility of our `viewDidLoad` method is simply to create the peripheral manager. We'll also be conscientious and ensure that when our app enters the background, we stop broadcasting. We'll do this by observing the `UIApplicationDidEnterBackgroundNotification` event of default `NSNotificationCenter` and calling our `stopBroadcasting` method when the event is observed.

Add the `viewDidLoad` method now:

```
-(void)viewDidLoad {
    [super viewDidLoad];

    self.peripheralManager = [[CBPeripheralManager alloc]
      initWithDelegate:self queue:nil];

    [[NSNotificationCenter defaultCenter] addObserver:self
      selector:@selector(stopBroadcasting:)
      name:UIApplicationDidEnterBackgroundNotification
      object:nil];
}
```

[ 76 ]

*Chapter 4*

In order to start advertising our beacon data, we need to implement the `peripheralManagerDidUpdateState` method of the `CBPeripheralManagerDelegate` protocol; when the Bluetooth peripheral is powered up, we can start advertising.

This is just like we did back in *Chapter 3, Broadcasting Advertisements – Sending Offers*, but this time we will ensure not to use an old iOS device that doesn't have BLE capability. If this occurs, we'll show an alert view.

We determine that a device doesn't have BLE capability when `CBPeripheralManager` reports a state of `CBPeripheralManagerStateUnsupported`.

Now, add the detection implementation:

```
-(void)peripheralManagerDidUpdateState:(CBPeripheralManager 
  *)peripheral {
    if (peripheral.state == CBPeripheralManagerStateUnsupported) {
        UIAlertView * av = [[UIAlertView alloc]
           initWithTitle:@"Error" message:@"This device doesn't 
           support BLE" delegate:self cancelButtonTitle:@"Close" 
           otherButtonTitles:nil, nil];

        [av show];
        return;
    }

    if (peripheral.state == CBPeripheralManagerStatePoweredOn) {
        // Start broadcasting.
        CLBeaconRegion * beaconRegion = [[CLBeaconRegion alloc] 
           initWithProximityUUID:[[NSUUID alloc] 
           initWithUUIDString:@"A547414E-C4D6-4778-BBEB-
           57BA3BD679E2"] identifier:@"Treasure"];

        NSNumber * power = [NSNumber numberWithInt:-63];

        NSMutableDictionary * sData = [beaconRegion 
           peripheralDataWithMeasuredPower:power];

        [self.peripheralManager startAdvertising:sData];
    }
}
```

[77]

Finally, if our iOS device is too old, we need to handle the alert view and dismiss the view controller:

```
-(void)alertView:(UIAlertView *)alertView
  clickedButtonAtIndex:(NSInteger)buttonIndex
{
    [self dismissViewControllerAnimated:YES completion:nil];
}
```

## Finally, wire it up

We need to wire the view up to the view controller; our view only needs two subviews: an image to show our lovely treasure and a button to dismiss it.

Create your view so that it looks like the following figure, and bind the button to the `stopBroadcasting` action:

Our treasure view controller view

## Building the hunter view controller

The hunter view controller is where all the fun happens. Once we enter the beacon region, we need to start ranging for beacons and then monitor our distance from the first beacon that we range in the collection.

*Chapter 4*

Let's have a quick look at how our user interface should look for `LIHunterViewController` from the following figure:

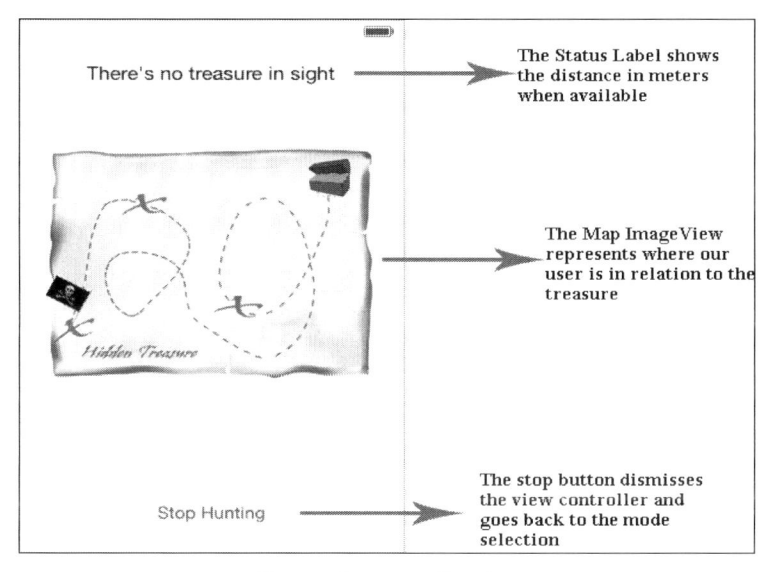

Hunter view controller view

## Hunter view controller states

Our hunter view controller has a number of states based on the distance from the beacon.

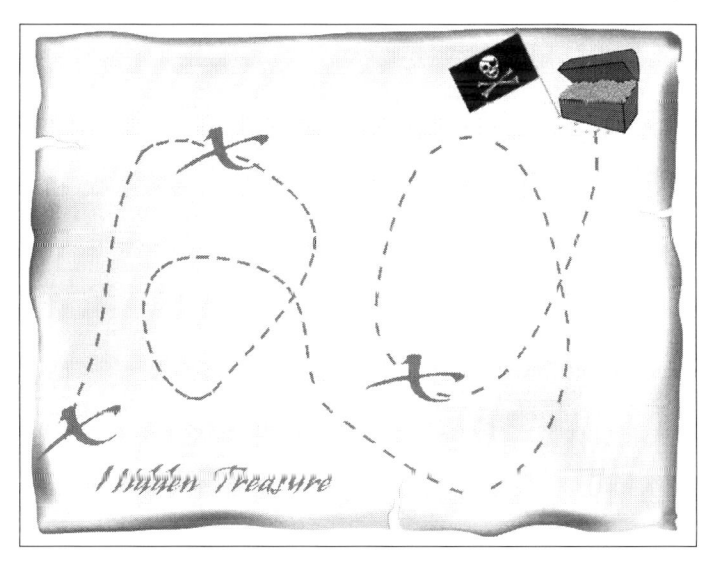

Hunter view controller states

**[ 79 ]**

*Ranging Beacons – Hunting for Treasure*

The following table describes the states of these properties:

| Distance from beacon | Map image | Status label text |
| --- | --- | --- |
| `CLProximityUnknown` | `Treasure-Map-1.png` | There's no treasure in sight |
| `CLProximityFar` | `Treasure-Map-2.png` | The treasure is very far away (%.2fm) |
| `CLProximityNear` | `Treasure-Map-3.png` | The treasure is very close (%.2fm) |
| `CLProximityImmediate` | `Treasure-Map-4.png` | We've found the treasure |

Once we get within half a meter of our beacon, we'll show an alert with the message **You found the treasure**, and then we'll dismiss the view controller since we don't need to search anymore. It makes sense that `LIHunterViewController` needs to handle the alert view. We also need `CLLocationManager` to range our beacons, so we need to handle the delegate methods for this object too.

## Imports and public properties

Let's start by setting up our interface in the `LIHunterViewController.h` file.

Add the declarations to your view controller for both `CLLocationManagerDelegate` and `UIAlertViewDelegate`:

```
#import <UIKit/UIKit.h>
#import <CoreBluetooth/CoreBluetooth.h>
#import <CoreLocation/CoreLocation.h>

@interface LIHunterViewController : UIViewController<CLLocationManagerDelegate, UIAlertViewDelegate>

@property (nonatomic, strong) IBOutlet UILabel * statusLabel;
@property (nonatomic, strong) IBOutlet UIImageView * mapImageView;

@end
```

## Private properties

Let's set up our private properties. We'll need `CLLocationManager` to range the beacons and `CLBeaconRegion` to represent the region that we're ranging.

*Chapter 4*

Add these properties to the private interface declaration in `LIHunterViewController.m`:

```
@interface LIHunterViewController ()
@property (nonatomic, strong) CLLocationManager * locationManager;
@property (nonatomic, strong) CLBeaconRegion * beaconRegion;
@end
```

## Loading the view

Our `CLHunterViewController` needs to do a few things when it's loading:

1. Instantiate its `CLLocationManager` instance.
2. Ask for permission to use the user's location.
3. Create a `CLBeaconRegion` instance representing the region.
4. Set itself as the delegate for the region.
5. Start ranging the beacons within the region.

Let's create our `viewDidLoad` method to perform these actions now:

```
-(void)viewDidLoad{
    [super viewDidLoad];

    // Create a new location manager.
    self.locationManager = [[CLLocationManager alloc]
      init];
    // Ask for location permission.
    [self.locationManager requestAlwaysAuthorization];

    // Create a new region.
    self.beaconRegion = [[CLBeaconRegion alloc]
      initWithProximityUUID:[[NSUUID alloc]
      initWithUUIDString:@"A547414E-C4D6-4778-BBEB-
      57BA3BD679E2"] identifier:@"Treasure"];

    [self.locationManager setDelegate:self];
    [self.locationManager
      startRangingBeaconsInRegion:self.beaconRegion];

}
```

## Entering and exiting the region

When we enter or exit a region, we need the start and stop ranging beacons.

Add the following `CLLocationManagerDelegate` methods:

```
-(void)locationManager:(CLLocationManager *)manager
  didEnterRegion:(CLRegion *)region
{
    [self.locationManager
      startRangingBeaconsInRegion:self.beaconRegion];
}

-(void)locationManager:(CLLocationManager *)manager
  didExitRegion:(CLRegion *)region {
    [self.locationManager
      stopRangingBeaconsInRegion:self.beaconRegion];
}
```

## Changing the state

To change between the states shown in the figure of the *Building the hunter view controller* section, we need to set the map image and status message when our beacons are ranged. In order to do this, we need to implement the `locationManager:didRangeBeacons:inRegion` method of the `CLLocationManagerDelegate` protocol.

The following code shows the method in its entirety; we'll break it down line by line in a moment.

For now, add the code to your implementation:

```
-(void)locationManager:(CLLocationManager *)manager
  didRangeBeacons:(NSArray *)beacons inRegion:(CLBeaconRegion
  *)region {

    if (beacons.count == 0) return;

    CLBeacon * beacon = [beacons firstObject];

    NSString * imageName;
    NSString * message;
    bool showAlert = false;

    switch (beacon.proximity) {
        case CLProximityFar:
            imageName = @"Treasure-Map-2.png";
```

```
          message = [NSString stringWithFormat:@"The treasure is
            very far away (%.2fm)", beacon.accuracy];
          break;
        case CLProximityNear:
          imageName = @"Treasure-Map-3.png";
          message = [NSString stringWithFormat:@"The treasure is
            very close (%.2fm)", beacon.accuracy];
          break;
        case CLProximityImmediate:
          imageName = @"Treasure-Map-4.png";
          message = @"We've found the treasure!!!";
          showAlert = true;
          break;
        case CLProximityUnknown:
        default:
            imageName = @"Treasure-Map-1.png";
            message = @"There's no treasure in sight";
            break;
    }

    [self.mapImageView setImage:[UIImage imageNamed:imageName]];
    [self.statusLabel setText:message];

    if (showAlert)
    {
        [self.locationManager
           stopRangingBeaconsInRegion:self.beaconRegion];
        UIAlertView * av = [[UIAlertView alloc]
           initWithTitle:@"Well done!"
        message:@"You found the treasure"
        delegate:self cancelButtonTitle:@"Stop hunting"
           otherButtonTitles:nil, nil];

        [av show];
    }
}
```

Since we called the `startRangingBeaconsInRegion` method before we entered the region, we might actually be passed an empty array in this method. In this scenario, we don't need to do anything, so we can return out of the method:

```
    if (beacons.count == 0) return;
```

*Ranging Beacons – Hunting for Treasure*

Next, we need to pull the first beacon from the array. In our use case, there's only one treasure. If you're building other apps, there might be lots of beacons in this array:

```
CLBeacon * beacon = [beacons firstObject];
```

Using the beacon proximity value, we gather values for the image and label using the switch statement before setting the view values:

```
NSString * imageName;
NSString * message;
bool showAlert = false;
switch (beacon.proximity) {
    ...
}
[self.mapImageView setImage:[UIImage imageNamed:imageName]];
[self.statusLabel setText:message];
```

Finally, if our proximity to the beacon is `CLProximityImmediate`, we show our alert view, congratulating the user on finding the treasure:

```
if (showAlert)
    {
        [self.locationManager stopRangingBeaconsInRegion:self.beaconRegion];
        UIAlertView * av = [[UIAlertView alloc] initWithTitle:@"Well done!"
            message:@"You found the treasure"
            delegate:self cancelButtonTitle:@"Stop hunting"
            otherButtonTitles:nil, nil];

        [av show];
    }
```

To dismiss the controller when our alert view is shown, we need to implement the `UIAlertViewDelegate` protocol's `alertView:clickedButtonAtIndex:` method to dismiss the view controller when the alert is tapped.

Add the alert view now:

```
-(void)alertView:(UIAlertView *)alertView
   clickedButtonAtIndex:(NSInteger)buttonIndex
{
    [self dismissViewControllerAnimated:YES completion:nil];
}
```

## Tidying up

Just like in our treasure view, we need a method to tidy up and dismiss our view controller. This time, we need to stop ranging beacons using the following steps:

1. Add the `stopHunting` method, shown as follows:

   ```
   - (IBAction)stopHunting:(id)sender {
       [self.locationManager
          stopRangingBeaconsInRegion:self.beaconRegion];
       [self dismissViewControllerAnimated:YES completion:nil];
   }
   ```

2. Wire this action to the `touchUpInside` event of the button in the view.

> Again, don't forget the iPad storyboard too!

## Being extra conscientious

We should ensure that we're tidying up if the app enters the background.

Add an observer to the `stopHunting:` method when the app enters the background:

```
[[NSNotificationCenter defaultCenter] addObserver:self
   selector:@selector(stopHunting:)EnterBackgroundNotification
object:nil];
```

## Completing the code

Debug and test your app on two devices. Start the app on one device and start running it as the treasure. Try to get at least 50 meters away before starting hunter mode on the second device.

Slowly move towards your treasure and see the map and messages change before you get less than an arm's length away. Once you do this, your hunter should show an alert view and then close when dismissed.

## Summary

In this chapter, we expanded our knowledge of the `CLLocationManager` and `CLBeacon` classes by determining our device distance from a beacon using the `CLBeacon` class's proximity and accuracy properties.

In the next chapter, we'll discuss beacon discovery when our app is in the background, and using this knowledge, we'll be building a proximity-based dating app.

Since there's a lot of code in this chapter, you might come across some stumbling blocks; feel free to ask me any questions on Twitter at `@craiggilchrist` (`https://twitter.com/craiggilchrist`).

# 5
# Detecting Beacons in the Background – Location Dating

So far, we have talked about discovering beacons, ranging beacons, and even using our iOS device to broadcast as a beacon. You should be feeling pretty empowered right now. All of these use cases, however, require your app to be *running*.

Having a running app for every use case isn't realistic. Considering that iBeacons are basically triggers for functionality, it makes sense that some of this functionality might be to bring the app into the foreground. In this chapter, we'll explore some other use cases where the app might be running in the background and is brought to life when a beacon region is entered.

To demonstrate background beacon detection, we'll create a location-based dating app that notifies the user when a potential date is nearby.

We'll cover the following topics:

- Monitoring for beacons in the background
- iOS architecture to defer region monitoring to the operating system
- Different scenarios for background monitoring
- Configurations needed for background monitoring
- Using beacons with passbook

# Real-life use cases

If you think about it, most usages of iBeacons won't always involve the app running in the foreground. Most apps are most likely to be awakened when entering the boundaries of a beacon region and then brought into the foreground by the user if they want to use the app.

# An example use case for retail loyalty

Imagine that you're building an app for retail loyalty. In this scenario, you are almost certainly going to want to trigger some functionality when the user comes into the range of your store. You might want to send the customer a tasty offer for your new bagel range, or simply offer users loyalty cards just in case they want to pop in for coffee.

# An example use case for airline assistance

Now, ponder building an app for an airline. Your app allows users to book their flight and download their boarding pass. The app also allows the user to get departure lounge discounts and directs them around the airport.

Once you book your flight using the app, it becomes completely useless until you arrive at the airport. During this time, your user forgets about it; he/she doesn't need its features until he/she approaches the airport terminal. In this scenario, you want to present the user with their boarding pass as they approach the check-in desk. The user opens the app and presents the boarding pass to the check-in staff.

Now, your user checks their bags and is stress-free; they are ready to do some shopping. As the user approaches the departure lounge, you present them with a push notification describing the fantastic offers available. The user opens the app, reviews the offers, and decides to head over to buy some new headphones from the electronic goods store to make their flight a little more comfortable.

These are just two examples of when your app is more likely to be *awakened* by beacons.

It's very rare that you won't want to know when your user is in the range of one of your beacons and is not using the app. This is why Apple, in its infinite wisdom, has made it very easy to monitor for regions in the background.

# Handing over responsibility

In iOS, regions (`CLBeaconRegion` or `CLRegion`) associated with your app are tracked all the time, including when the app isn't running. If a region boundary is crossed while an app isn't running, the app is relaunched in the background to handle the event.

Similarly, if the app is suspended when the event occurs, it's woken up and given a short amount of time (around 10 seconds) to handle the event.

When necessary, an app can request more background execution time using the `beginBackgroundTaskWithExpirationHandler:` method of the `UIApplication` class.

This means that your app can perform a few actions such as showing a local notification or sending an HTTP request (or both), but it can't really perform running actions such as ranging beacons any longer; this is because once your app goes back to sleep, this function is stopped being called.

You can perform longer running actions in the background by turning on the background modes in the **Capabilities** tab of the application in Xcode, as shown in the following figure. Turning on background modes adds the `Required Background Modes` key to the `info.plist` file.

> If you don't have a very valid reason for requiring constant location updates in your commercial application, then Apple is likely to reject the application during review because of the implications on battery life.

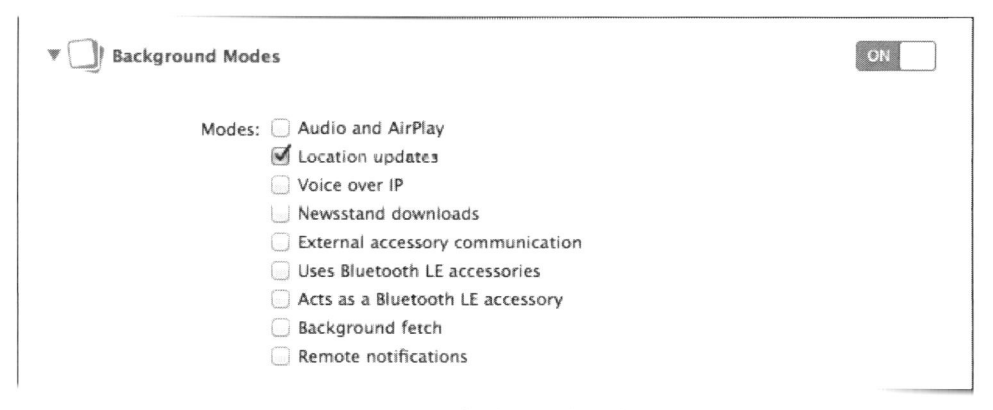

Turning on background modes

Realistically, you don't need to turn on background modes for iBeacon-powered apps. This feature is reserved for apps that need location for navigation, such as the Waze app (https://www.waze.com/) that allows you to continue navigating to your journey in the background with local notifications for turn-by-turn instructions.

When you create `CLLocationManager` and call the `startMonitoringForRegion` method, your app starts receiving events for the specified region. When your app enters the background, it hands this responsibility over to the OS.

While your app is running, all `CLLocationManager` events related to beacons such as `didRangeBeacons:inRegion:` are handled directly by the delegate from `CLLocationManager`. When your app runs once and enters the background, the events are *deferred* to the operating system; this fires up your application to handle the events, which in turn brings your app to the foreground for a short period.

## The CLBeaconRegion options

The properties of the `CLBeaconRegion` instance have a huge impact on how your app behaves when running in the background. Let's explore a few of these options now:

- `CLBeaconRegion.notifyOnEntry`: When this property is YES, a device crossing from the outside to the inside of the region triggers the delivery of a notification. If the property is NO, a notification is not generated. If the app is not running when a boundary crossing occurs, the system launches the app in the background to handle it.

- `CLBeaconRegion.notifyOnExit`: This property works in a similar way as mentioned in the preceding point, except for the notification that occurs when the device crosses from the inside to the outside of the region. There is usually a delay of up to 10 seconds after the device has fallen out of range of the last beacon in the region, but this can also be up to 30 seconds. This *cushion* time is to ensure that numerous entered and exited events are not called in quick succession while the user is traveling close to the edge of the boundary.

- `CLBeaconRegion.notifyEntryStateOnDisplay`: While `notifyOnEntry` and `notifyOnExit` are both actually inherited properties of `CLRegion`, `notifyEntryStateOnDisplay` is a `CLBeaconRegion` property in its own right. When set to YES, the location manager sends beacon notifications when the user turns on the display and the device is already inside the region. For the most responsive background notifications, always set the `CLBeaconRegion.notifyEntryStateOnDisplay` property to YES. This ensures that the app comes into the foreground when the screen is turned on even if the device is on the lock screen.

In some scenarios, you might want to show a notification when you enter a region, but only when the user is looking at their device. In this scenario, you should set `notifyOnEntry` to `NO` and `notifyEntryStateOnDisplay` to `YES`, which will notify the region entry only when the device display is on.

## Passbook integration

Wouldn't it be great if beacons worked directly with Apple's e-wallet solution passbook? Of course it would, and of course Apple has thought of this. You can easily bring your passbook passes to the foreground when in the range of a beacon.

As of iOS 7.0, Apple added the beacon dictionary keys to the PassKit bundle, giving the ability to define activating beacons alongside text to display when in the range of a particular beacon.

With the new dictionary values, you can specify an array of beacons that show a message and a thumbnail image of the pass, which allows you to bring the pass to the forefront without unlocking your phone, as shown in the following figure:

Showing passbook passes from the lock screen using iBeacon

*Detecting Beacons in the Background – Location Dating*

Exploring PassKit (Apple's tool to create passes) is definitely beyond the scope of this book, so we'll only skim over the structure of a pass. It's enough to know that a pass is made up of a ZIP file with the file extension `.pkpass`, which contains the following files:

- The `pass.json` file that gives the pass details in JSON format, including the pass type, colors, titles, labels, and descriptions represented in the pass
- The icons and strip images used within the pass, which are in PNG format
- Developer signatures and certificates used within the pass

The `pass.json` file has a number of new beacon dictionary keys to allow your pass to be shown on the lock screen. These are shown in the following table:

| Key name | Type | Description |
| --- | --- | --- |
| `proximityUUID` | String | The UUID for your beacon region. |
| `major` | 16-bit unsigned integer | The major value of the beacon. |
| `minor` | 16-bit unsigned integer | The minor value of the beacon. |
| `relevantText` | String | This is optional. It is the text displayed on the lock screen when the pass is currently relevant. For example, it could be a description of the nearby location, such as "**Store nearby on 1st and Main**". |

In order to show you how this functionality works, I created a pass to use in the tutorial, which includes the following beacon array in its `pass.json` file:

```
{
    … //rest of pass.json omitted for clarity
    "beacons": [
        {
            "proximityUUID": "B20891ED-02C7-4987-AE14-
              2DB2D759F735"",
            "major": 2,
            "minor": 1,
            "relevantText": "A hot guy is nearby"
        },
        {
            "proximityUUID": "B20891ED-02C7-4987-AE14-
              2DB2D759F735",
            "major": 1,
            "minor": 1,
```

```
            "relevantText": "A hot gal is nearby"
        }
    ]
}
```

> Passbook and PassKit are beyond the scope of this book, but if you want a great tutorial on creating passbook passes using PassKit, I recommend Marin Todorov's two-part tutorial on Ray Wenderlich's site `http://bit.ly/rw-passbook`.

# Our tutorial app

We will now create an app that demonstrates all of these features; it will monitor regions in the background before presenting a local notification. When the app is running, we'll range the beacons in our region and stop ranging them when the app drops into the background. Finally, we'll allow the user to add a **Ticket to love** passbook event ticket pass that will show up on the lock screen when it's within a region.

To test our app, we'll use the companion OS X application to advertise one of two beacons, representing either a "hot guy" or a "hot gal".

# The scenario

You've been asked to build a new location-based dating app. When lonely hearts sign up to the service, they are sent an iBeacon key ring that they carry around with them, and they also get to download a companion app that lets them know when other lonely hearts are in the area.

The lonely heart key rings use the same UUID; however, hot gals broadcast the major value of 1 while hot guys broadcast the major value of 2. Each lonely heart will be given a unique minor value; however, you've been asked to test the concept using just one guy and one gal value, as shown in the following table:

| UUID | Major | Minor | Lonely heart |
|---|---|---|---|
| B20891ED-02C7-4987-AE14-2DB2D759F735 | 1 | 1 | A hot gal |
|  | 2 | 1 | A hot guy |

Our user will be able to choose whether they're seeking a hot guy or a hot gal. When the app is running, they'll be shown the distance in meters from their target date, if one is in range.

*Detecting Beacons in the Background – Location Dating*

When the app is in the background and the user comes into range of a beacon, they'll be shown a push notification telling them that a potential date is in range. If the app is open, ranging of the beacons will begin.

Finally, the user will also be able to add a passbook pass to their device, which will show them whenever a guy or gal is in region; we'll call this the "ticket to love".

## Viewing anatomy

We will produce an app that looks like the one shown in the following figure. The app will be a single view application, and again, we'll use a storyboard to create our user interface.

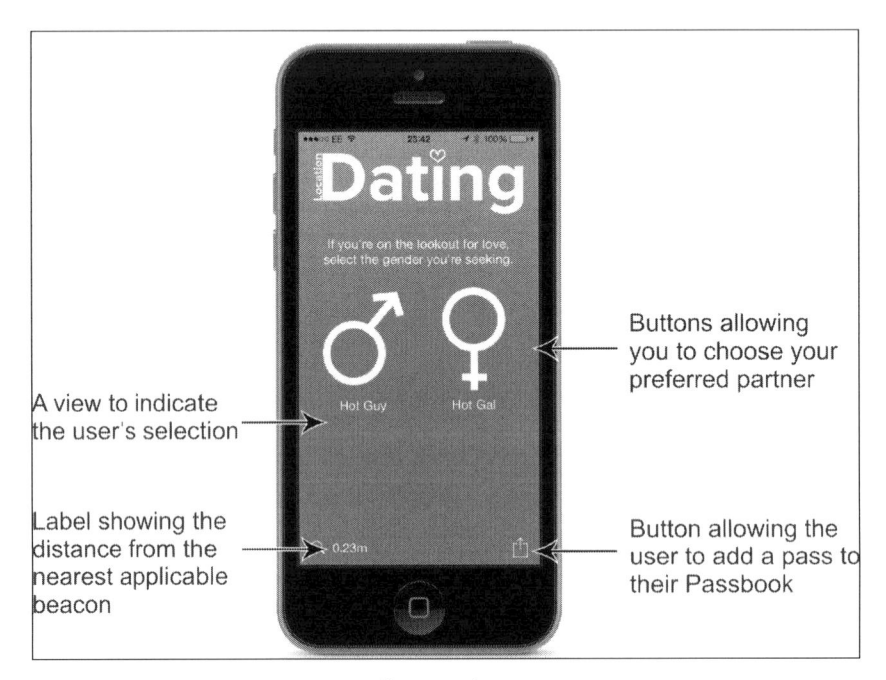

Our app view

All of the images used in this app are contained within the chapter code. There's also a very important file named `hotdate.pkpass`, which is the signed passbook pass associated with the tutorial; be sure to download them all.

# The code

We'll build our app in two parts. All of the beacon functionality we need will be done in the app delegate (`LIAppDelegate`) while our app will consist of a single view controller.

We'll communicate between the app delegate and `ViewController` using the default `NSNotificationCenter`.

## Creating the application

Let's begin by creating the project and adding the frameworks. There's quite a lot of code in this tutorial, so we'll go through each piece step by step:

1. Fire up Xcode and create a single view application. When prompted, use the following options for your new product, as follows:
    - **Product Name**: `Location Dating`
    - **Organization Name**: `Learning iBeacon`
    - **Company Identifier**: `com.learning-ibeacon`
    - **Class Prefix**: `LI`
    - **Devices**: `iPhone`

2. We need the `CoreLocation` and `PassKit` frameworks for this app. Go ahead and add these frameworks now as we did in the previous chapters.

3. Next, we need to ensure that our app has the plist settings to enable it to ask for location permission. Add the `NSLocationAlwaysDescription` key to the info tab of the project settings. Set the value to **This app needs your permission to find a hot date**.

## Creating the view

Again, we use storyboards for this app. By creating a single view application, we've already been given `LIViewController`, and a storyboard with this controller has already been represented.

I won't go into detail about how to create each control in the storyboard since we covered much of this in the previous chapters. Consider the following steps for creating the view:

1. Open the `Main.storyboard` file and lay out your view as shown in the *Our app view* figure. For the items at the bottom, I used UIToolbar with a flexible Space bar button item to separate the `distance` label from the action button.

> If you want to jump straight to the code, then feel free to *borrow* the view from the complete code that is available to download.

2. Create the following properties in `LIViewController.h` and wire them up in the storyboard. The `highlightView` property is used to show the user which button has been selected; the rest of the properties should be pretty obvious, but again, do refer back to the completed code if you're not sure:

   ```
   @property (weak, nonatomic) IBOutlet UIButton * guyButton;
   @property (weak, nonatomic) IBOutlet UIButton * galButton;
   @property (weak, nonatomic) IBOutlet UIView *
     highlightView;
   @property (weak, nonatomic) IBOutlet UILabel * guyLabel;
   @property (weak, nonatomic) IBOutlet UILabel * galLabel;
   @property (weak, nonatomic) IBOutlet UIBarButtonItem *
     distanceBarButtonItem;
   ```

3. Open `LIViewController.m` and create the following method, then wire the `touchUpInside` action from both `guyButton` and `galButton` to the method. We'll complete the implementation later:

   ```
   -(IBAction)genderButtonPressed:(id)sender {
   }
   ```

4. Add another method for the action button in the toolbar at the bottom of the view and wire up the action to it. Again, we'll provide the implementation later:

   ```
   -(IBAction)actionButtonPressed:(id)sender {
   }
   ```

## Configuring the app delegate

Our app delegate is responsible for all of the beacon functionalities and is the host (and delegate) of our `CLLocationManager` instance. Consider the following steps to configure the app delegate:

1. Open `LIAppDelegate.h` and add the import for `CoreLocation`:

   ```
   #import <CoreLocation/CoreLocation.h>
   ```

2. Since our app delegate needs to be `CLLocationManagerDelegate`, add the declaration to the interface declaration, location manager instance, and beacon region so that our interface declaration looks like this:

   ```
   @interface LIAppDelegate : UIResponder
     <UIApplicationDelegate, CLLocationManagerDelegate>
   ```

*Chapter 5*

```
@property (strong, nonatomic) UIWindow * window;
@property (strong, nonatomic) CLLocationManager *
  locationManager;
@property (strong, nonatomic) CLBeaconRegion *
  beaconRegion;

@end
```

3. We'll need a way for our view controller to tell the location manager in our app delegate to start monitoring for "guys" or "gals". Add the following method declaration:

   ```
   -(void)startMonitoringForMajor:(NSInteger)major
     minor:(NSInteger)minor{
   }
   ```

4. Since we're looking at our custom method, let's create the implementation now. Open `LIAppDelegate.m` and clear out all of the default methods. Create the method stub for the `startMonitoringForMajor:minor:` function:

   ```
   -(void)startMonitoringForMajor:(NSInteger)major
     minor:(NSInteger)minor {
   }
   ```

5. Within the `startMonitoringForMajor:minor:` method, we need to check whether we have a location manager yet. Add this code to check and create the `CLLocationManager` instance and ask for permission:

   ```
   if (!self.locationManager) {
      self.locationManager = [[CLLocationManager alloc]
        init];
      [self.locationManager requestAlwaysAuthorization];
      self.locationManager.delegate = self;
   }
   ```

6. Next, we need to stop monitoring the existing beacon region if it exists. Straight after the last line of code, add this check:

   ```
   if (self.beaconRegion) {
      [self.locationManager
        stopMonitoringForRegion:self.beaconRegion];
      [self.locationManager
        stopRangingBeaconsInRegion:self.beaconRegion];
   }
   ```

## Detecting Beacons in the Background – Location Dating

7. Now, we need to create `CLBeaconRegion`. This time, we won't use a generic region, we'll look for a very specific beacon based on what the view controller has requested. Add the region instantiation after the previously added line:

   ```
   NSUUID * uuid = [[NSUUID alloc]
     initWithUUIDString:@""B20891ED-02C7-4987-AE14-
     2DB2D759F735""];

   // Create a new region.
   self.beaconRegion = [[CLBeaconRegion alloc]
     initWithProximityUUID:uuid major:major minor:minor
     identifier:@""Hot Date""];
   ```

8. We need our all-important beacon region properties. We want to show a push notification when we enter or exit a region when the app is in the background, regardless of whether the device display is on. Set the properties of the beacon and then request `CLLocationManager` to start monitoring and ranging the beacons straight after the previous line. Normally, you will only start ranging beacons in a region once you know you're actually in the region, using the `locationManager:didEnterRegion` method. However, for this app, the other beacons are moving around, and so, we range straightaway:

   ```
   self.beaconRegion.notifyEntryStateOnDisplay = YES;
   self.beaconRegion.notifyOnEntry = YES;
   self.beaconRegion.notifyOnExit = YES;

   self.locationManager

   [self.locationManager
     startMonitoringForRegion:self.beaconRegion];
   [self.locationManager
     startRangingBeaconsInRegion:self.beaconRegion];
   ```

## No ranging in the background

Remember that there isn't much point in ranging beacons when our app is running in the background. Let's add `applicationDidEnterBackground` and `applicationDidBecomeActive` to stop and resume ranging the beacons.

Add the following methods to the `LIAppDelegate.m` file:

```
-(void)applicationDidEnterBackground:(UIApplication *)
  application {
    if (self.beaconRegion) {
      [self.locationManager
        stopRangingBeaconsInRegion:self.beaconRegion];
```

```
        }
    }

    -(void)applicationDidBecomeActive:(UIApplication *)
       application {
        if (self.beaconRegion) {
            [self.locationManager
               startRangingBeaconsInRegion:self.beaconRegion];
        }
    }
```

## Entering and exiting regions

We handled starting and stopping the monitoring of beacons when we're in the background, which means the only thing left to do is send a local notification when our app enters or exits a region, but only if the app is running in the background.

We want to present a local notification with a message that is relevant to the users' search (guys or gals), and so we'll need to determine this from the major value of the current region. Consider the following steps to enter and exit regions:

1. Add the `locationManager:didEnterRegion:` delegate method to the app delegate:

    ```
    -(void)locationManager:(CLLocationManager *)manager
       didEnterRegion:(CLRegion *)region {

        if ([[UIApplication sharedApplication]
           applicationState] == UIApplicationStateBackground) {

            UILocalNotification * notification =
               [[UILocalNotification alloc] init];
            if ([self.beaconRegion.major intValue] == 1) {
                notification.alertBody = @""A hot gal is
                   nearby"";
            }
            else {
                notification.alertBody = @"A hot guy is
                   nearby";
            }
            notification.soundName =
               UILocalNotificationDefaultSoundName;
            notification.applicationIconBadgeNumber = 1;
            [[UIApplication sharedApplication]
               presentLocalNotificationNow:notification];
        }
    }
    ```

2. Similarly, when we exit a region, we want to send a notification to the user to tell them that they missed out on a date. Add the `locationManager:didExitRegion:` method to the app delegate:

```
-(void)locationManager:(CLLocationManager *)manager
   didExitRegion:(CLRegion *)region {

     if ([[UIApplication sharedApplication]
       applicationState] == UIApplicationStateBackground) {

        UILocalNotification * notification =
          [[UILocalNotification alloc] init];
        notification.alertBody = @"You've lost track of
          the hot date";
        notification.soundName =
          UILocalNotificationDefaultSoundName;
        notification.applicationIconBadgeNumber = -1;
        [[UIApplication sharedApplication]
          presentLocalNotificationNow:notification];
    }
}
```

## Clearing out badges

Did you notice that we presented the local notification with a badge in the `locationManager:didEnterRegion` delegate method? I'm quite fanatical about clearing out every badge on my iPhone, and I know I'm not alone.

Let's add the `application:didFinishLaunchingWithOptions:` method to clear out these pesky badges:

```
- (BOOL)application:(UIApplication *)application
  didFinishLaunchingWithOptions:(NSDictionary *)launchOptions
{
    [UIApplication sharedApplication].applicationIconBadgeNumber
      = 0;
    return YES;
}
```

## Ranging beacons

Finally, we need to range beacons, and when we do, we need a way to notify the view controller that a beacon distance has changed. To do this, we'll use `NSNotificationCenter` and a custom notification named `DistanceUpdated`. When sending our custom notification, we'll pass the beacon itself as the object, which we can pick up in our observer method in the view controller that we'll implement shortly.

Add the `locationManager:didRangeBeacons:inRegion` delegate method to our app delegate:

```
-(void)locationManager:(CLLocationManager *)manager
  didRangeBeacons:(NSArray *)beacons inRegion:
  (CLBeaconRegion *)region
{
    if ([beacons count] == 0) return;

    CLBeacon * beacon = [beacons firstObject];

    [[NSNotificationCenter defaultCenter]
       postNotificationName:@""DistanceUpdated"" object:beacon];
}
```

## Implementing our view controller

We have finished with our app delegate and got method stubs for most of our view controller methods. We're in great shape; all we need to do now is implement a couple of view controller features and we'll be done.

### Initializing the view

We will use a nice gradient pink image for the background of our view. When our app first loads, the user doesn't select a preference, and so, we need to hide `highlightView` and set a default message for the `distanceBarButtonItem` controls. Consider the following steps for initializing the view:

1. Add the `Background.png` image to the project.

2. Then, add the following code to the `viewDidLoad:` method of the `LIViewController.m` file to initialize the view controls:

   ```
   self.view.backgroundColor = [UIColor
     colorWithPatternImage:[UIImage
     imageNamed:@"Background.png"]];
   [self.distanceBarButtonItem setTitle:@"Not searching"];
   [self.highlightView setHidden:YES];
   ```

3. Under memory constraints, our app might have its memory reclaimed. When our view loads, we need to check whether our app delegate has a beacon region, and if it does, we simulate a button press to configure the view. First, add the import for the app delegate at the top of `LIViewController.m`:

   ```
   #import "LIAppDelegate.h"
   ```

4. Then, add the following code to the end of the `viewDidLoad` method:

   ```
   LIAppDelegate * delegate = (LIAppDelegate*)
     [UIApplication sharedApplication].delegate;

   if (delegate.beaconRegion) {
       if ([delegate.beaconRegion.major intValue] == 1) {
           [self genderButtonPressed:self.galButton];
       }
       else {
           [self genderButtonPressed:self.guyButton];
       }
   }
   ```

5. We should also clean up the view when it first appears by setting the label value. Add the following `viewDidAppear:` method:

   ```
   -(void)viewDidAppear:(BOOL)animated {
       [super viewDidAppear:animated];
       [self.distanceBarButtonItem setTitle:@"Not searching"];
   }
   ```

## Receiving beacon distance

Remember that our app delegate is in charge of the beacon location and ranging and that it sends this information on using a custom notification named `DistanceUpdated`. Consider the following steps for receiving beacon distance:

1. Add a new observer method to `LIViewController.m`. This method will accept our beacon range event and use the accuracy property of the beacon to set the distance bar button item title:

   ```
   - (void) receiveDistance:(NSNotification *) notification
   {
       CLBeacon * beacon = notification.object;

       self.distanceBarButtonItem.title = [NSString
         stringWithFormat:@"%.2fm", beacon.accuracy];
   }
   ```

2. Add a couple of lines to the `viewDidLoad` method to observe our custom notification:

   ```
   [[NSNotificationCenter defaultCenter] removeObserver:self];

   [[NSNotificationCenter defaultCenter] addObserver:self
     selector:@selector(receiveDistance:)
     name:@"DistanceUpdated" object:nil];
   ```

## Choosing a gender

It's time to fill in our `genderButtonPressed:` method. Within it, we should check whether the guy or gal button has been pressed and then tell our app delegate to start monitoring for the relevant major and minor values.

We also need to set our highlight view frame to sit underneath the selected button by following the given steps:

1. Complete the `genderButtonPressed:` method so that it looks like the following code:

   ```
   -(IBAction)genderButtonPressed:(id)sender {
       [self.distanceBarButtonItem setTitle:@"Searching..."];
       [self.highlightView setHidden:NO];

       LIAppDelegate * delegate =
          (LIAppDelegate*)[UIApplication
          sharedApplication].delegate;

       CGRect highlightFrame = self.highlightView.frame;

       int major = 0;

       if (sender == self.guyButton) {
           major = 2;
           highlightFrame.origin.x =
              self.guyLabel.frame.origin.x +
              (self.guyLabel.frame.size.width*.5) -
              (highlightFrame.size.width*.5);
       }
       else {
           major = 1;
           highlightFrame.origin.x =
              self.galLabel.frame.origin.x +
              (self.galLabel.frame.size.width*.5)
              (highlightFrame.size.width*.5);
       }

       self.highlightView.frame = highlightFrame;

       [delegate startMonitoringForMajor:major minor:1];
   }
   ```

2. The following line of code sets the frame to be positioned in the middle of guyLabel:

   ```
   highlightFrame.origin.x = self.guyLabel.frame.origin.x +
     (self.guyLabel.frame.size.width*.5) -
     (highlightFrame.size.width*.5);
   ```

## Adding a passbook pass

Finally, we need to implement the actionButtonPressed: method to add our pass to passbook. Execute the following steps:

1. From the downloaded resources, add the hotdate.pkpass file to your project.

2. Add an import declaration to the top of the LIViewController.m file to add PassKit:

   ```
   #import <PassKit/PassKit.h>
   ```

3. Finally, add the implementation for the actionButtonPressed method. The method needs to present a new PKAddPassesViewController, which presents a view controller, allowing the user to add a pass to their passbook:

   ```
   - (IBAction)actionButtonPressed:(id)sender {
   
       NSString * filePath = [[NSBundle mainBundle]
         pathForResource:@"hotdate" ofType:@"pkpass"];
       
       NSData * fileData = [NSData
         dataWithContentsOfFile:filePath];
       
       PKPass * hotDatePass = [[PKPass alloc]
         initWithData:fileData error:nil];
       
       PKAddPassesViewController * vc =
         [[PKAddPassesViewController alloc]
         initWithPass:hotDatePass];
       
       [self presentViewController:vc animated:YES
         completion:nil];
   }
   ```

## Testing your application

We have finished building the app, and it's time to test. There's a lot of code in this tutorial, so don't be disheartened if it doesn't work the first time.

*Chapter 5*

# Testing the beacons

Just go through the steps again to see where you went wrong, or review the complete code from the download resources. Use the following steps:

1. Tap **guyButton** before pressing the device's home button, thus sending the app to the background.

2. Now, using the companion OS X app, start the beacon entitled **Chapter 5: The hot guy**, as shown in the upcoming figure. You should be presented with a push notification.

3. Start the app, and you should see the distance being updated in **distanceBarButtonItem**.

4. Press the home button again before turning off the beacon in the companion app.

5. Wait for up to 15 seconds for the exit region event to fire, and again, you should be presented with a different push notification notifying you that you've exited the region.

6. Perform steps 1 to 5 for the gal.

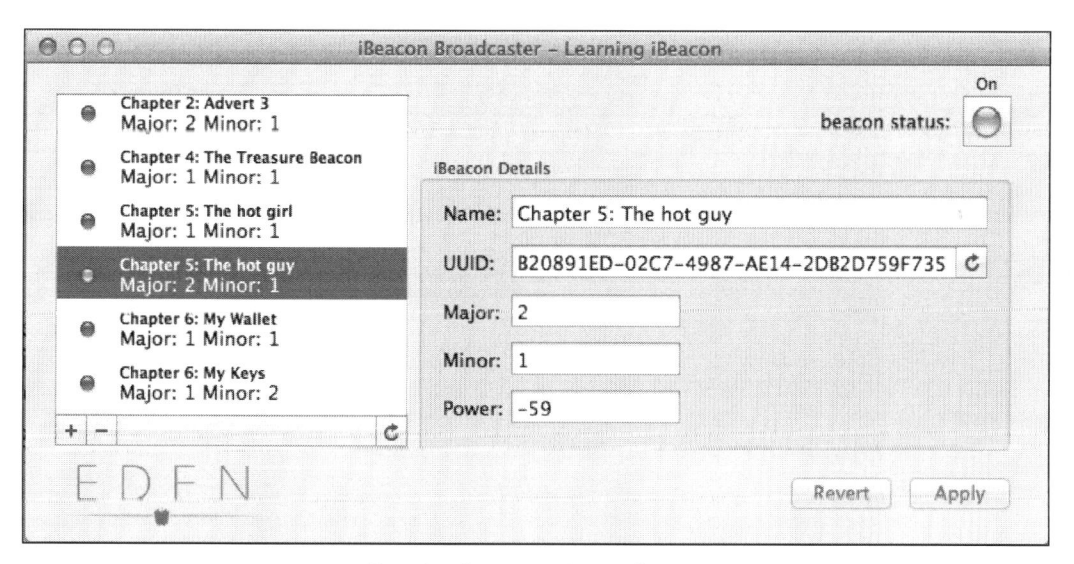

Running the companion application

# Testing the passbook pass

Testing the passbook pass is simple. Start by pressing the **Action** button. You should be presented with a view controller, allowing you to add the pass to your passbook; do so.

[ 105 ]

Finally, lock your device and open the lock screen before turning on the beacon profile in the companion app. Your lock screen should look something like the *Showing passbook passes from the lock screen using iBeacon* figure. When you slide across on the notification, you are presented with the pass without having to unlock your device.

# Summary

Congratulations, you're now an iBeacon guru. In this chapter, we completed our knowledge of `CLBeaconRegion` and its properties, which affect background behaviors such as `notifyEntryStateOnDisplay` and `notifyOnEntry`.

We discussed the limitations of functionality when our app is activated by an OS when entering a region, and why we shouldn't range beacons in the background.

We also discovered how we can bring the passbook passes to the front of the lock screen using iBeacons.

In the next chapter, we'll expand our knowledge of what to do when we leave a region, and we'll discuss home automation and the implications of iBeacon upon that field.

# 6
# Leaving Regions – Don't Forget Your Stuff

So far, we have mostly discussed about the triggering functionality when your device enters a region from beacons that are static. However, that's not always going to be the case. Beacons, after all, are tiny Bluetooth devices that can be easily ported around with you.

One of the areas in which iBeacon technology offers an exciting opportunity is **home automation**. Very inexpensive computing power such as the Raspberry Pi (`http://www.raspberrypi.org/`) and innovative projects such as Ninja Blocks (`https://ninjablocks.com/`) are being funded by Kickstarter, which means that there is a growing community of people subscribing to the Internet of Things.

Beacons not only offer an excellent opportunity to trigger functionality based on your proximity to space in the world, but also gives you the ability to trigger notifications and features when items come into your range because beacons don't need to be fixed to bricks and mortar.

I'm sure if you're anything like me, you'll have a set of three or four things that go with you everywhere. For me, these things are my wallet, my house keys, and also, my Boston Terrier, Stitch, who comes to the office with me every day. Wouldn't it be great if you got a notification when those things aren't nearby?

In this chapter, we'll be learning:

- How to use background modes to allow ranging beacons in the background
- How to trigger functionality when a beacon gets further than two meters away even when your app is running in the background
- About the usage of iBeacon in home automation

Before we get started, let's touch on some of the other technologies that make home automation an amazing subject for the implementation of iBeacon.

## Raspberry Pi

Raspberry Pi is a credit-card-sized computer that outputs high-resolution displays via HDMI and includes USB and Ethernet interfaces. It does everything you'd expect a desktop computer to do and also has a hackable circuitry.

The model A retails at $ 25 while B+ retails at $ 35, making it an incredible, hackable, affordable, and most of all, an accessible little device. The Pi has rekindled the hobbyist programmer and led to a whole host of home automation projects. Check out the latest Raspberry Pi home automation projects on the Raspberry Pi Foundation blog (http://bit.ly/pi-ha).

## Ninja Blocks

Ninja Blocks started out as a Kickstarter project with the intention of connecting your physical world with the **World Wide Web (WWW)**. The Kickstarter funding smashed its initial crowd-sourcing goals, and has since then shipped thousands of Ninja Blocks devices.

The platform is controlled by simple *if this, then that* style tasks using effectors and actuators. Both effectors and actuators can be made up in the physical or virtual world, which means you can do things such as post on Twitter when a door sensor is triggered by an opening door or turn on a lava lamp when a file is uploaded to Dropbox.

Find out more about Ninja Blocks on their official website at http://bit.ly/ninja-blocks.

## Nest

The Nest project is a learning thermostat that controls your home's central heating system and learns about your habits to ensure that your home is always at the optimum temperature while also saving energy when you're not home.

Nest was recently acquired by Google who maintained its open platform API, allowing us programmers to continue to build solutions to work with it.

Find out more about the Nest API on the nest developer website at http://bit.ly/nestapi.

# Phillips Hue

Phillips Hue is a network-enabled lighting system for your home. You swap all the bulbs in your home with Hue LED bulbs and configure the Hue bridge as a control hub for all of the bulbs in your home, giving you a completely personalized colored lighting depending on any factor you choose. You can change your lighting's color to red to match the creepy horror movie in the middle of the movie while your partner has a blue light in the bathroom to enable them to enjoy a nice relaxing bath.

The developer APIs allow you to trigger bulb configurations via HTTP posts, which means that you can automate almost any lighting situation you like using web hooks. You can trigger flashing red lights when there's breaking news on your favorite news channel or light the living room blue when you're mentioned on Twitter.

Find out more about the Hue API at the developer website at `http://bit.ly/dev-hue`.

# Belkin WeMo

The Belkin WeMo switch is a programmable, Wi-Fi-enabled power switch that plugs directly into your power outlet and in which you plug your mains-powered devices into. The Belkin Wi-Fi-enabled WeMo switch lets you turn electronic devices on or off from anywhere. The WeMo switch uses your existing home Wi-Fi network to provide wireless control of TVs, lamps, stereos, heaters, fans, and more.

Find out more about the WeMo API at the developer website at `http://bit.ly/devwemo`.

# iBeacon and home automation

You might be asking yourself where iBeacon fits into all of these amazing projects, and the answer is *everywhere*! What makes all of these projects so incredibly successful is their open platforms, which means that as an iOS developer with an iPhone or iPad, the world is your oyster.

My team at my company, Eden Agency, likes to play with the Internet of Things. Since we're a team of app developers, we like to get our hands dirty hacking at anything hackable, and this means I've been fortunate enough to get my hands on lots of technologies that are making waves in home automation.

A great middleware piece of hardware is the Ninja Block since it simplifies the interfacing between devices. By using Ninja Blocks, you can automatically wire up Belkin WeMo devices and Phillips Hue devices as actuators for any of your triggers, including web hooks.

*Leaving Regions – Don't Forget Your Stuff*

By setting up a web hook, you can effectively trigger interactions in your home by doing a simple HTTP post request from your iPhone when you come into range of a beacon. Using a single Ninja Block, you can have your coffee machine turn on, the lights set to relax, and music start playing as you drive up your street after a tough day at the office.

This can be done using simple web hooks and your custom iOS app by following these simple steps:

1. You enter the region of a beacon situated on your garage door. This beacon has a broadcast range of 70 m, so your iPhone picks up the region at the end of your street.
2. Your app is opened by the OS and the `locationManager:didEnterRegion` method is called on your `CLLocationManagerDelegate` instance.
3. Your delegate method sends a HTTP post request to a Ninja Block inbound web hook.
4. The web hook triggers a Ninja Block rule. This rule simultaneously triggers the following actions:
    1. Turn on the Belkin WeMo attached to the coffee machine.
    2. Turn on the Belkin WeMo attached to the stereo.
    3. Send the RGB value 135, 206, 250 to the living room and kitchen end points on the Phillips Hue device to set the lights to blue.

This can all be achieved by configuring one simple rule using Ninja Blocks, and by writing no more than a few lines of code to send a HTTP request.

# Beacon stickers

A number of companies are now developing iBeacon stickers that allow you to flip the idea of beacons being static and you being the variable position to the consideration that things in the real world can move and your device can trigger functionality based on that moving device.

For example, imagine that you want to track every place you've cycled using an iPhone that uses a cycling tracker app. Your app doesn't know the difference between when you're riding a bus, jogging, or cycling, and so would rely on you to tell it when you're cycling, which you are likely to forget at least once.

If you had a very small sticker, such as a beacon, attached to your bicycle, you could automatically start tracking your journey when you're on your bike without having to think about it.

Estimote and Jaalee are the two companies that have streamlined stickers such as beacons for exactly the kind of purpose I just described. Estimote Nearable beacons provide additional functionality including temperature and accelerometer data, while the Jaalee ES003 model even boasts a long battery life due to *electro-magnetic energy harvesting*, which sounds a bit like science fiction to me.

Beacon stickers are the perfect solution to cases that require the geolocation of *things* rather than just you.

# Our tutorial

We're going to demonstrate this sticker-type functionality by building an app that lets you add beacon profiles to a local database, and when the beacon is more than two meters away, the app shows a push notification.

Our companion app already includes three beacon profiles for the important things we might forget, which are listed in the following table:

| UUID | Major | Minor | |
|---|---|---|---|
| C5FAC3DE-33D5-469C-B094-AD527AF3ECCD | 1 | 1 | My wallet |
| | | 2 | My keys |
| | | 3 | My dog |

The idea behind our app is that we never leave anything important behind. This means that we need to send a notification if the app isn't active and a beacon moves out of range or present an alert if the app is running at the time we lose the beacon.

# Ranging beacons in the background

Since all beacons share the same UUID, we can't rely on the `locationManager:didExitRegion` delegate method because if we've got two out of the three important things with us, then we'll still be in the region and so we might leave something behind and not be notified! We'll need to rely on the `locationManager:didRangeBeacons:inRegion` delegate method to tell us when we've lost a beacon.

"Wait, didn't you say that ranging beacons in the background isn't possible back in *Chapter 4, Ranging Beacons – Hunting for Treasure?*" I hear you say...

Technically, ranging beacons in the background isn't possible. You can activate the app when entering and exiting regions, but your app is brought into the foreground by these delegate methods. You've only got around 4 to 5 seconds of time before the app goes back to sleep; at this point, the `locationManager:didRangeBeacons:inRegion` method stops running.

*Leaving Regions – Don't Forget Your Stuff*

# Tracking locations using background modes

In some circumstances, you may want to track your location in the background as if you've got a navigation app that doesn't need to be in the foreground to give you directions such as Google Maps or the Waze app. In these scenarios, Apple has kindly provided us with background modes, which strictly speaking aren't meant for iBeacon implementations.

By checking the **Location updates** option from the **Background Modes** option in the **Capabilities** tab of our Xcode project, we tell the compiler that our app needs some extra special permissions to run permanently in the background. This can be seen in the following screenshot:

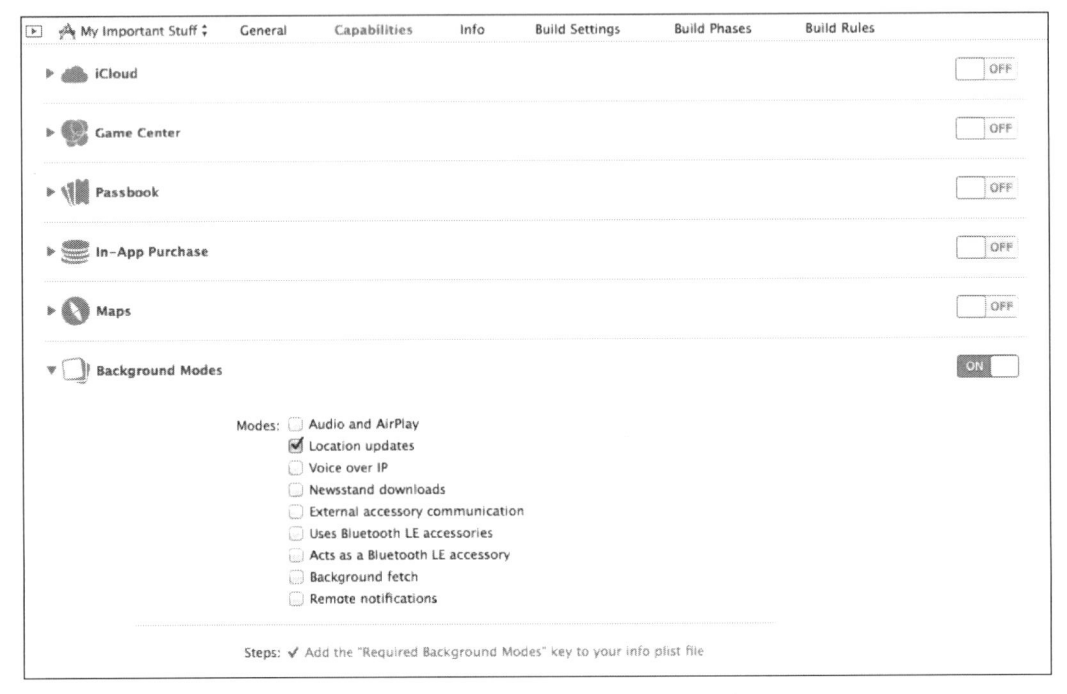

Location updates enabled in background modes

By turning on the location updates, you still won't be able to receive ranged beacons in the background because strictly speaking, this option isn't intended for iBeacon implementation.

[ 112 ]

## Cheating the system

To receive ranged beacon information in the background, we need to cheat. We need to use one of the `CLLocationManager` traditional location methods that are allowed to be run in the background (`startUpdatingLocation`). Once we call `startUpdatingLocation`, our location manager is already tracking location and keeping our app running in the background, and therefore, we're also receiving ranged beacon information at the same time in our `locationManager:didRangeBeacons:inRegion` delegate method.

> I can almost guarantee that if you attempt to use this technique in a production app to be released via the App Store, it will fail its review. Apple doesn't take apps that drain the battery, and so by constantly tracking a user's location without any functionality that requires it will result in a failed review.

# Building our app

Let's get started with building our "important stuff" app. We'll be using core data to store a list of our important stuff, and luckily, Apple has provided a very nice template, which should give us a head start. Consider the following steps:

1. Fire up Xcode and create a new project. This time, choose **Master-Detail Application** as your project template and call the project `My Important Stuff`. Be absolutely sure to check the **Use Core Data** option as this tutorial heavily relies on it.

2. We're going to need `CoreLocation`; so, add that to the linked frameworks and libraries as we've done in previous chapters.

## Beginning the app with a database schema

Let's start with the database required to support the app. We'll need to store all of our beacons within the local database so that our location manager knows what's missing. We'll also need to remove any of the default entities that the template has created so that we don't cloud up our nice clean code. Consider the following steps:

1. Open up the `My_Important_Stuff.xcdatamodel` file. This file contains the meta descriptions of our database.

2. Delete the `Event` entity, which has been created by default, and add a new entity named `Beacon`.

*Leaving Regions – Don't Forget Your Stuff*

3. Add three new attributes to the beacon as follows; your model should look like the following screenshot:
   - **major**: **Integer 16**
   - **minor**: **Integer 16**
   - **name**: **String**

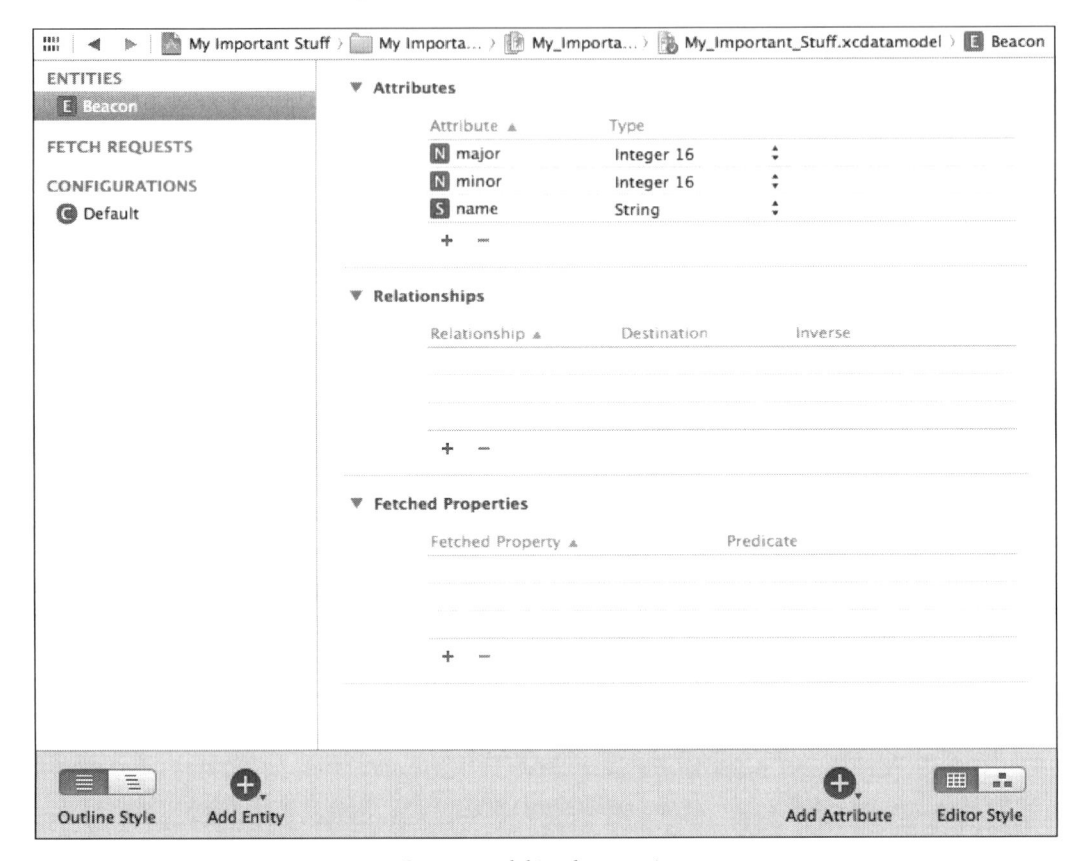

Beacon model implementation

## Using a little helper

We will do some duplicate functionality across both `LIMasterViewController` and `LIDetailViewController`, and so, it makes sense to share these in a helper class.

Our helper class needs the following methods:

- `+(NSString*)proximityStringForBeacon:(CLBeacon*)beacon`: This method returns a string representing the distance from the device such as Near or Far

[ 114 ]

- `+(NSString*)stringForBeacon:(CLBeacon*)beacon`: This method returns a string representation of a beacon in the `major:minor:proximity` format and is used for comparing beacons
- `+(NSArray*)beaconsNearbyForBeacons:(NSArray*)beacons`: This method filters an array of beacons to only those that have a proximity status of `CLProximityNear` or `CLProximityImmediate`

In order to add these methods, follow the given steps:

1. Create a new Objective-C class and a subclass named `NSObject`. Name this class `LIBeaconHelper`.

2. Open `LIBeaconHelper.h` and add the static method declarations:

   ```
   +(NSString*)proximityStringForBeacon:(CLBeacon*)beacon;
   +(NSString*)stringForBeacon:(CLBeacon*)beacon;
   +(NSArray*)beaconsNearbyForBeacons:(NSArray*)beacons;
   ```

3. Open `LIBeaconHelper.m` and add the implementation of these methods:

   ```
   +(NSString*)proximityStringForBeacon:(CLBeacon*)beacon {
       NSString * proximity;

       switch (beacon.proximity) {
           case CLProximityFar:
               proximity = @"Far";
               break;
           case CLProximityImmediate:
               proximity = @"Immediate";
               break;
           case CLProximityNear:
               proximity = @"Near";
               break;
           case CLProximityUnknown:
           default:
               proximity = @"Unknown";
               break;
       }

       return proximity;
   }

   +(NSString*)stringForBeacon:(CLBeacon*)beacon {
       NSString * proximity = [self
         proximityStringForBeacon:beacon];
   ```

*Leaving Regions – Don't Forget Your Stuff*

```objc
        return [NSString stringWithFormat:@"%@:%@:%@",
           beacon.major, beacon.minor, proximity];
    }

    +(NSArray*)beaconsNearbyForBeacons:(NSArray*)beacons {

        NSArray * nearbyBeacons = [beacons
           filteredArrayUsingPredicate:[NSPredicate
           predicateWithFormat:@"proximity >= %d",
           CLProximityNear]];

        return [NSArray arrayWithArray:nearbyBeacons];

    }
```

4. So that we don't need to import the helper class twice, it's best to add it to the precompiled header class. Open the `My Important Stuff-Prefix.pch` file and add the import:

   `#import "LIBeaconHelper.h"`

## Master view controller implementation

Next, we'll build our master view controller. This class is going to be responsible for showing a list of all my beacons and their range if known. It'll also be the host for the location manager functionality. Although our template has created lots of code in the `LIAppDelegate` class to support core data, we won't actually be using it:

1. Open `LIMasterController.h` and add an import for `CoreLocation` as we've done in previous chapters.

2. Add two new properties for our location manager and region, shown as follows:

   ```objc
   @property (strong, nonatomic) CLLocationManager
      *locationManager;
   @property (strong, nonatomic) CLBeaconRegion *beaconRegion;
   ```

3. Add `CLLocationManagerDelegate` to the `LIMasterViewController` class declaration, as this time, our master view will be acting as the delegate.

4. We're going to need a couple more private properties. We need one property for keeping the beacons that our location manager has ranged and then another to show when we last notified our user that they've gone out of range of their items (since we don't want to be bombarding them with alerts).

[ 116 ]

5. Open `LIMasterController.m`, and in the interface declaration, add the following new properties:

   ```
   @property (strong, nonatomic) NSArray *beacons;
   @property (strong, nonatomic) NSDate *lastNotification;
   ```

## Configuring the view controller

Our `viewDidLoad` method requires us to configure the location manager and regions, and is also going to be the point of call to start ranging for beacons. Consider the following steps:

1. Within the `viewDidLoad` method, right after the call to `[super viewDidLoad]`, add the following code to tidy up any existing location manager:

   ```
   // Restart the location manager.
   if (self.locationManager) {
      [self.locationManager
         stopMonitoringForRegion:self.beaconRegion];
      [self.locationManager stopUpdatingLocation];
      [self.locationManager
         stopRangingBeaconsInRegion:self.beaconRegion];
   }
   ```

2. Now, we need to create the location manager and ask for permission. We also need to configure the associated region and then start monitoring the beacons. Immediately after the last code that you have added, add the following code:

   ```
   self.locationManager = [[CLLocationManager alloc] init];
   self.locationManager.delegate = self;
   [self.locationManager requestAlwaysAuthorization];

   self.beaconRegion = [[CLBeaconRegion alloc]
      initWithProximityUUID:[[NSUUID alloc]
      initWithUUIDString:@"C5FAC3DE-33D5-469C-B094-
      AD527AF3ECCD"] identifier:@"My Stuff"];

   [self.locationManager
      startRangingBeaconsInRegion:self.beaconRegion];
   ```

3. Remember our hack to ensure we can range the beacons in the background? Add a call to the location manager to start updating the location:

   ```
   [self.locationManager startUpdatingLocation];
   ```

*Leaving Regions – Don't Forget Your Stuff*

4. Since we're getting the user's location constantly and not actually using it, we should make it as battery-efficient as possible. To do this, we can set the desired accuracy of the location manager to a very large region, which will reduce the GPS usage and ultimately increase the battery life:

   ```
   self.locationManager.desiredAccuracy =
     kCLLocationAccuracyThreeKilometers;
   ```

## Fetching data from the Core Data framework

Core Data provides ways to persist data easily using a local database stored on the device. When using Core Data, you as the application developer define the object graph mapping and simply choose the way the data is stored; Core Data then handles the complexity of managing the database schema and you manage data using entity descriptions and very simple queries.

Using Core Data allows you to choose how your persistent data store is implemented. This could be XML, atomic, or most commonly using a bundled SQLite database, which is then copied to the application storage on the first run. To get a better understanding of Core Data, there is an excellent article on the developer library documentation available from Apple at http://bit.ly/ios-coredata.

> XML isn't available as a data store on iOS, but is included as an option for Core Data when developing apps for OS X.

Our master-detail application template with core data uses a single table of Events by default. We've already removed the Event entity from the model and replaced it with our Beacon entity, but now we need to ensure that what the app pulls back is what we're expecting to see. Consider the following steps:

1. Scroll down to the `fetchedResultsController` method and find the line that creates `NSEntityDescription`. It should look like this:

   ```
   NSEntityDescription *entity = [NSEntityDescription
     entityForName:@"Event"
     inManagedObjectContext:self.managedObjectContext];
   ```

2. Replace it with the entity name in this line so that it looks like this:

   ```
   NSEntityDescription *entity = [NSEntityDescription
     entityForName:@"Beacon"
     inManagedObjectContext:self.managedObjectContext];
   ```

3. The template has created sort descriptors, which sort the results based on `timeStamp`. We want to sort our database results by the beacon's major and minor values. Replace the `NSSortDescriptor` declarations with our own code:

```
// Edit the sort key as appropriate.
NSSortDescriptor *majorSortDescriptor = [[NSSortDescriptor
    alloc] initWithKey:@"major" ascending:YES];
NSSortDescriptor *minorSortDescriptor = [[NSSortDescriptor
    alloc] initWithKey:@"minor" ascending:YES];
NSArray *sortDescriptors = @[majorSortDescriptor,
    minorSortDescriptor];
```

## Configuring the table cell

Our table cell needs to represent the major and minor values and our beacon name, and currently, the prototype cell has a basic style that doesn't give us much room to present our beacon data:

1. Open the `Main.storyboard` file and find the `MasterViewController` view. Select the prototype cell and change its style to **Left Detail** within **Attributes Inspector**.

2. Now that we've got the **Left Detail** style in our prototype cell, we can make use of both the `textLabel` and `detailTextLabel` properties to show our beacon data. Scroll down to the `configureCell:atIndexPath:` method and remove its current implementation body.

3. First, we need the managed object from Core Data for the index path. Add the following line:

```
NSManagedObject *object = [self.fetchedResultsController
    objectAtIndexPath:indexPath];
```

4. We're going to use `detailTextLabel` to show the beacon major, minor, and name values in the `major:minor - name` format. For example, the beacon attached to my dog takes the format `1:3 - My Dog`. Add the following line to set the cell text from the managed object properties.

```
cell.detailTextLabel.text = [NSString
    stringWithFormat:@"%@:%@ - %@", [object
    valueForKey:@"major"], [object valueForKey:@"minor"],
    [object valueForKey:@"name"]];
```

# Leaving Regions – Don't Forget Your Stuff

5. Our `textLabel` property is going to show the current distance from the device using our helper method. To find out the distance, we will need to see if there's an associated beacon that has been ranged by our location manager. If not, we'll need to show "Unknown". Add the code to loop through our beacons and set the values if the app knows the location of our managed object:

```objc
for (CLBeacon * beacon in self.beacons) {
    int major = [[object valueForKeyPath:@"major"]
        intValue];
    int minor = [[object valueForKeyPath:@"minor"]
        intValue];
    
    if ([beacon.major intValue] == major && [beacon.minor
        intValue] == minor) {
        cell.textLabel.text = [LIBeaconHelper
            proximityStringForBeacon:beacon];
        return;
    }
}

cell.textLabel.text = @"Not found";
```

## Notifying the user

We need a method to notify the user when their important things aren't in range anymore. When the app is active, we want to show a UIAlert, and when the app isn't active, we'll present a local notification.

Add the following method to send the notification:

```objc
-(void)notifyUser {
    
    // Build the string of missing stuff.
    NSString * message = @"Hey dude, your important stuff
        isn't nearby!";
    
    if ([UIApplication sharedApplication].applicationState ==
        UIApplicationStateActive) {
        UIAlertView * alert = [[UIAlertView alloc]
            initWithTitle:@"Missing Stuff"
            message:message delegate:nil
            cancelButtonTitle:@"Ok"
            otherButtonTitles:nil, nil];
        
        [alert show];
    }
```

```
    else {
        UILocalNotification * localNotification =
          [[UILocalNotification alloc] init];
        [localNotification setAlertBody:message];
        [localNotification
          setSoundName:UILocalNotificationDefaultSoundName];
        [[UIApplication sharedApplication]
          presentLocalNotificationNow:localNotification];
    }
}
```

## Inserting new objects

The template has created an `add new object` button for us that has its `touchUpInside` event bound to the `insertNewObject` method. This method is still trying to set the `timeStamp` property. We need to set default values for a new beacon.

Scroll to the `insertNewObject:` method and replace the line `[newManagedObject setValue:[NSDate date] forKey:@"timeStamp"];` with the following code:

```
[newManagedObject setValue:@"My new beacon" forKey:@"name"];
    [newManagedObject setValue:[NSNumber numberWithInt:1]
      forKey:@"major"];
    [newManagedObject setValue:[NSNumber numberWithInt:1]
      forKey:@"minor"];
```

## Ranging beacons

The last major thing to do is range the beacons within our master view controller. Consider the following steps:

1. Create the empty method stub:

    ```
    -(void)locationManager:(CLLocationManager *)manager
      didRangeBeacons:(NSArray *)beacons
      inRegion:(CLBeaconRegion *)region {
    }
    ```

2. Within the new method, the first thing we need to do is filter our beacons to only those that are immediate or near to the device using our helper method. Declare a new variable and filter the beacons that have been ranged:

    ```
    NSArray * nearbyBeacons = [LIBeaconHelper
      beaconsNearbyForBeacons:beacons];
    ```

[ 121 ]

3. We don't want to bombard our user with alerts; we only want to notify them every 5 minutes if their stuff isn't in range. For this, we'll use the last notification property, and if it hasn't been set, then we'll set it to 300 seconds ago (5 minutes):

   ```
   if (!self.lastNotification) self.lastNotification =
     [NSDate dateWithTimeIntervalSinceNow:-300];
   ```

4. Next, we need to determine whether the beacons are what we expected to retrieve; if not, we need to notify our user that some of their stuff is missing:

   ```
   id <NSFetchedResultsSectionInfo> sectionInfo =
     [self.fetchedResultsController sections][0];
   int expectedItems = (int)[sectionInfo numberOfObjects];

   if (expectedItems != [self.beacons count] &&
     [self.lastNotification timeIntervalSinceNow] < -300)
     {
       [self notifyUser];
       self.lastNotification = [NSDate date];
     }
   ```

5. Finally, we need to set the locally stored beacons array and refresh our table so that it can update the distance of our beacons:

   ```
   self.beacons = nearbyBeacons;
   [self.tableView reloadData];
   ```

# Detailed view controller implementation

Our detail view controller is responsible for editing managed object data. Its sole responsibility is to set the name, major, and minor values of the beacon in the Core Date database.

Our master view controller creates new beacons using the **add** button. When any beacon is selected in the master view's table, the master view controller hands the managed object over to the detail view controller.

Before we head off and create our detail view, there's one thing left that we've got to do. When our master view reappears (after our detail view is dismissed), we need to save the changes to the database. This way, what our detail view really does is that it just sets the three properties of an existing object:

1. Add the following method to `LIMasterViewController.m`:

   ```
   -(void)viewWillAppear:(BOOL)animated {
       [self.managedObjectContext save:nil];
   }
   ```

2. Our detail view is going to need `UITextField` properties for the three fields. Open `LIDetailViewController.h` and add the following properties:

   ```
   @property (weak, nonatomic) IBOutlet UITextField
     *majorTextField;
   @property (weak, nonatomic) IBOutlet UITextField
     *minorTextField;
   @property (weak, nonatomic) IBOutlet UITextField *
     nameTextField;
   ```

3. Our controller also needs to be the delegate for these new text fields; so, let's add `UITextFieldDelegate` to our class declaration so that it looks like this:

   ```
   @interface LIDetailViewController :
     UIViewController<UITextFieldDelegate>
   ```

## Configuring the view

Our view needs three simple text fields with three labels. Each of the text fields should set our detail view controller object as the reference and should be bound to the associated properties as created in the previous steps.

Create your view so that it looks like the following screenshot:

Our Detail view

## Getting and setting properties

The template we used has already created a `configureView` method for us. Let's replace the body to use our beacon item instead of the default event item:

```objc
- (void)configureView
{
    if (self.detailItem) {

        self.nameTextField.text =  [[self.detailItem
            valueForKey:@"name"] description];

        self.majorTextField.text =  [[self.detailItem
            valueForKey:@"major"] description];

        self.minorTextField.text =  [[self.detailItem
            valueForKey:@"minor"] description];
    }
}
```

When our view controller is dismissed, we need to set the values from our text fields back to the object. Add the following implementation of `viewWillDisappear`:

```objc
- (void)viewWillDisappear:(BOOL)animated {
    [super viewWillDisappear:animated];

    if (self.isMovingFromParentViewController) {

        NSNumberFormatter * f = [[NSNumberFormatter alloc] init];
        [f setNumberStyle:NSNumberFormatterNoStyle];

        [self.detailItem setValue:self.nameTextField.text
            forKey:@"name"];
        [self.detailItem setValue:[f
            numberFromString:self.majorTextField.text]
            forKey:@"major"];
        [self.detailItem setValue:[f
            numberFromString:self.minorTextField.text]
            forKey:@"minor"];
    }
}
```

## Validating input

We need to validate the user entry to ensure that the major and minor values aren't greater than what int16 will allow and also that they haven't entered whitespace for the name. Add the following `UITextFieldDelegate` method to validate the input:

```
-(void)textFieldDidEndEditing:(UITextField *)textField {
    if (textField == self.majorTextField || textField ==
      self.minorTextField){
        if ([textField.text intValue] > INT16_MAX) {
            textField.text = [NSString stringWithFormat:@"%i",
              INT16_MAX];
        }
        if ([textField.text intValue] < 1) {
            textField.text = @"1";
        }
        return;
    }

    if ([[textField.text
      stringByTrimmingCharactersInSet:[NSCharacterSet
      whitespaceCharacterSet]] length] == 0) {
        textField.text = @"My beacon";
    }
}
```

## Finishing off UI

We also need to finish off the UI properly so that we can press **next** on the same text field, and also so that we can resign any responders if the user touches outside of the text fields when a keyboard is showing. Consider the following points:

1. Add the following implementation to handle the `Next` button on the keyboard:

    ```
    -(BOOL)textFieldShouldReturn:(UITextField *)textField {

        if (textField == self.nameTextField)
          [self.majorTextField becomeFirstResponder];
        if (textField == self.majorTextField)
          [self.minorTextField becomeFirstResponder];

        return YES;
    }
    ```

2. Add the following touch event to resign responders:
   ```
   -(void)touchesBegan:(NSSet *)touches withEvent:(UIEvent
     *)event
   {
       [super touchesBegan:touches withEvent:event];
       [self.nameTextField resignFirstResponder];
       [self.majorTextField resignFirstResponder];
       [self.minorTextField resignFirstResponder];
   }
   ```

# Adding NSLocationAlwaysUsageDescription

As we've done in previous chapters, we need to add a description of the location usage, which is displayed in the location permission dialog. Under the target info settings dialog, add the NSLocationAlwaysUsageDescription key to **Custom iOS Target Properties**. Set the value to something like `This app requires access to your location to track your important items`.

# Enabling the background mode

The final thing to do is to enable the background mode for the app so that we can range beacons in the background. Consider the following steps:

1. Open the project settings and click on the **Capabilities** tab.
2. Turn the **Background Modes** option on.
3. Check the box next to **Location updates**.

*Enabling location updates in background mode*

# Testing your app

Test your app using the companion OS X app provided. Add a wallet, keys, and dog to your collection as shown in the *Location updates enabled in background modes* figure and then turn the beacon profiles on and off in the companion app to test the notifications. Remember to wait for 5 minutes before receiving your notifications.

# Summary

In this chapter, we learned about the amazing potential of iBeacons in home automation and also that beacons need not be fixed in the world. It's just possible for the beacon to be movable than the mobile user! Our tutorial showed us how to utilize background modes to range beacons in the background and also how to show local notifications when the app is in the background.

In the next chapter, we'll be discussing purchasing beacons from well-known manufacturers and their SDKs. We'll also be hacking Estimote beacons, which will require hardware beacons to complete the tutorial.

# 7
# Vendor SDKs – Buying and Configuring Beacons

In the previous chapters, we only utilized Apple's Core Location and Core Bluetooth frameworks to interact with beacons. Many vendors actually provide their own hardware beacons, a web-based API for managing beacons, and an SDK for manipulating their values over BLE.

In this chapter, we will explore Estimote beacons and the associated SDK and also ROXIMITY beacons before delving further into the ROXIMITY SDK and producing an app that allows you to configure the Estimote beacon UUID, major, and minor values.

## Estimote motes and SDK

Although Estimote have recently implemented a cloud-based platform, their beacons can quite happily work independent of it, and their beacons conform to the iBeacon specification as set out by Apple.

On top of the features laid out by the iBeacon specifications, Estimote beacons also include a temperature sensor and accelerometer for additional functionality.

Currently, the only data that is actually synchronized to the cloud is a property representing the color of the silicon case that surrounds the beacon and a single property signifying the beacon's location. This property is just intended as a reference for you as the beacon owner. When you purchase beacons from Estimote, they automatically add your beacons to the cloud platform.

## ROXIMITY implementation

ROXIMITY beacons implement a very different architecture. Although their beacon broadcasting ad rate is iBeacon certified, there is no way of actually choosing a UUID to suit your requirements.

ROXIMITY beacons are entirely cloud-platform managed. Much like Estimote, when you purchase ROXIMITY beacons, they are automatically added to your cloud account.

Since ROXIMITY beacons *must* use their SDK to build enterprise-level applications, it means that each beacon isn't locked down to a single UUID and so can be utilized for multiple apps.

ROXIMITY have based their platform very much on an advertiser network, and as such, their SDK allows you to implement rich notifications, modal pop ups, and pop up requests via simple web forms in their cloud platform without having to write any code.

By implementing the SDK, the ROXIMITY platform also gives you powerful targeting for your notifications based on demographics and behavior such as the dwell time.

## Choosing the best platform for your requirements

Although there are many more platforms than just the two we've discussed here, many implement similar architectures. If you're looking to build an enterprise-level advertising network and don't have the capability or resources to build a web platform, then ROXIMITY is the choice for you.

However, if you want more control over your beacon's implementation or want additional features beyond that of just the iBeacon specification, then Estimote or one of the other more open beacons is definitely a better choice.

You might have other considerations such as beacon size, cost, or branding of beacons. Check back to *Chapter 1, Welcome to iBeacon*, which gives a more in-depth run-down of some of the providers on the market at the time of writing.

## AltBeacon – the open beacon specification

Because there is no open and interoperable specification for proximity beacons, Radius Networks has authored the AltBeacon specification as a proposal on how to solve this problem. The AltBeacon specification defines the format of advertisement messages in an attempt to bring a standard platform-independent way for proximity beacons to broadcast.

This is unlike the iBeacon specification, which requires the vendor to register with Apple's MFI program in order to find out the exact Bluetooth advertising channel **protocol data unit** (**PDU**), which iOS devices look out for.

The AltBeacon specification defines the format of the advertisement message that BLE proximity beacons broadcast and is free for all to implement with no royalty or fees.

Keep an eye out for AltBeacon implementations. I'm sure they'll come thick and fast with third-party library implementations very soon.

# Using Estimote API 2.1

Our tutorial is going to take us through how to use the Estimote API to build an app, which allows us to configure Estimote beacons with custom UUID, major, and minor values.

To complete this tutorial, you will need some hardware. Estimote offer a 3-beacon developer kit at $ 99, which allows you to get started with building solutions using their beacons, which can be ordered from their website at https://order.estimote.com/.

I've used the latest SDK (2.1) at the time of writing this, but the developers working at Estimote are always busy and constantly improving their API and firmware. Before beginning this tutorial, I'd recommend heading over to the Estimote API pages (http://bit.ly/estimoteapi) and checking out the latest API.

I'd also recommend upgrading your Estimote beacon firmware to the latest version.

# Security

In the latest version of the Estimote SDK, you need to connect to the devices using the API app ID and API app token. When you buy beacons from Estimote, they're automatically added to the cloud platform (http://cloud.estimote.com/) and are secured from access using your personal keys.

When you try to connect to a beacon without authenticating, you will receive an authorization error. In order to connect to beacons to be configured, you need to have called the `setupAppID:andAppToken` static method of the `ESTBeaconManager` class previously, by providing your keys from the Estimote cloud.

# Estimote SDK classes

Estimote's API builds on top of the Core Location and Core Bluetooth frameworks, and many of the classes mimic and extend upon the functionality of Core Location.

We'll only be using two of the framework classes for this tutorial and their associated delegate protocols. For a comprehensive view of the API, head over to the website and read through their comprehensive documentation at http://bit.ly/estimote-github.

## ESTBeacon

The `ESTBeacon` class (as you've probably guessed) encapsulates a hardware beacon just like the `CLBeacon` class, but with a whole heap of extra properties and options. The `ESTBeacon` instances have many publicly available properties that you can access freely using the SDK, and then a number of properties that are only accessible once you've connected to the beacon.

Public properties of `ESTBeacon` are similar to those of the `CLBeacon` class including proximity UUID, major, minor, and RSSI.

Once you've connected to the beacon using the `connect` method, you also get access to the device's hidden properties, including (but not limited to):

- Battery level
- Remaining lifetime
- Battery type
- Whether the device is moving
- Firmware version

## ESTBeaconDelegate

The beacon delegate allows you to monitor for changes in the beacon's status, including connection and accelerometer changes. The delegate protocol includes four tasks:

- `beaconConnectionDidFail:withError::` This occurs when the connection to the device fails. This can be a transient fail and the app will still attempt connection.
- `beaconConnectionDidSucceeded::` This occurs when the connection to the device completes successfully and the connected functions are available.
- `beacon:didDisconnectWithError::` This occurs when the connection is broken, either intentionally (without error) or due to a fault in which the error is passed.

- `beacon:accelerometerStateChanged:`: This occurs when the accelerometer data has changed because the beacon is moving.

## ESTBeaconManager

The `ESTBeaconManager` class defines the interface for handling and configuring the Estimote beacons and getting related events to your application. You use an instance of this class to establish the parameters that describe the behavior of every beacon. You can also use a beacon manager object to retrieve all beacons in range.

Unlike `CLBeaconManager`, `ESTBeaconManager` allows you to discover beacons without a region. `ESTBeaconManager` mimics many of the `CLBeaconManager` methods for ranging and monitoring regions and also features for turning the device into a beacon.

`ESTBeaconManager` also includes methods that require Core Bluetooth for discovering Estimote beacons. We'll be using the `startEstimoteBeaconsDiscoveryForRegion:` method, which accepts a region but returns all Estimote beacons regardless of region if `nil` is passed.

## ESTBeaconManagerDelegate

The `ESTBeaconManagerDelegate` protocol mimics much of the `CLBeaconManager` methods and also provides event handlers for beacon discovery. We'll be using the `beaconManager:didDiscoverBeacons:inRegion:` method in our app.

# Let's get building

We'll be building a simple master-detail application similar to that of *Chapter 6, Leaving Regions – Don't Forget Your Stuff*. Our master view controller will be used to show the Estimote beacons in range, while the detail view controller will be used to change the values of the beacon.

Our detail view controller will also show the output from the beacon's temperature sensor and will also vibrate the iPhone when the beacon is moved.

Let's start by firing up Xcode and creating a new project following the given steps:

1. Choose **Master-Detail Application** as our template.
2. Set **Product Name** as `Estimote Beacon Manager`, uncheck the **Use Core Data** checkbox, and use LI as our class prefix.
3. To make our app vibrate, we will need the Audio Toolbox framework; so, go ahead and add that framework to the project.

## Adding EstimoteSDK

We'll be using CocoaPods to add EstimoteSDK. If you're not familiar with CocoaPods, it's a Ruby dependency manager for Objective-C projects that allows you to add dependencies and keep them up to date easily. Follow the given steps to add Estimote SDK:

1. Close your Xcode project and open a terminal window.

2. Navigate to your folder that contains the `xcodeproj` file. For example, you can navigate to the folder using the following command:

    ```
    cd //Users/craiggilchrist/Documents/Projects/Learning\ iBeacon/Estimote\ Beacon\ Manager
    ```

3. You'll need to ensure you've got CocoaPods and Ruby installed. If not, then run the following command. Be patient, it may take a little while:

    ```
    sudo gem install cocoapods
    ```

4. CocoaPods uses a plain text file named `Podfile` to determine its dependencies. Let's create and then open this text file now using the following command:

    ```
    touch Podfile
    nano Podfile
    ```

5. Now that `Podfile` is open in `nano`, add the following line to the file:

    ```
    pod 'EstimoteSDK', '~> 2.0'
    ```

6. Press *control* + *O* to save the file; when prompted, choose **Podfile** as the filename and press *enter*.

7. Press *control* + *X* to close the file.

8. Run the following command to install the dependencies. This may take a little while:

    ```
    pod install
    ```

9. This should have added all the dependencies required and created an `xcworkspace` file. From now on, we should only use the `xcworkspace` file to open our project. Since we have already got the terminal window open, we might as well use it to open our project again. Run the following command to open the project:

    ```
    open Estimote\ Beacon\ Manager.xcworkspace/
    ```

## Adding API access

Since we need to be authenticated to manage our beacons, we need to add a call to the `setupAppID:andAppToken:` method of `ESTBeaconManager` using our app ID, as follows:

1. Go to `http://cloud.estimote.com/#/account` and log in with your Estimote credentials.
2. Add the following code to `LIAppDelegate`, replacing the holding strings with your API credentials:

   ```
   - (BOOL)application:(UIApplication *)application
     didFinishLaunchingWithOptions:(NSDictionary
     *)launchOptions
   {
       [ESTBeaconManager setupAppID:@"<YOUR API APP ID>"
         andAppToken:@"<YOUR API APP TOKEN>"];
       return YES;
   }
   ```

## The helper class

Just like in *Chapter 6, Leaving Regions – Don't Forget Your Stuff*, we're going to create a little helper class. This time, its only responsibility is to return the color name of the beacon as returned from the cloud. Consider the following steps:

1. Create a new Objective-C class and name it `LIBeaconHelper`.
2. Add the method declaration to the header file:

   ```
   +(NSString*)colorNameForBeacon:(ESTBeacon*)beacon;
   ```

3. Add the implementation to the `LIBeaconHelper.m` file:

   ```
   +(NSString*)colorNameForBeacon:(ESTBeacon*)beacon {
       NSString * color = @"Unknown";
       switch (beacon.color) {
           case ESTBeaconColorBlueberry:
               color = @"Blueberry Pie";
               break;
           case ESTBeaconColorIce:
               color = @"Icy Marshmallow";
               break;
           case ESTBeaconColorMint:
               color = @"Cocktail Mint";
               break;
   ```

```
            case ESTBeaconColorTransparent:
                color = @"Transparent";
                break;
            case ESTBeaconColorWhite:
                color = @"Arctic White";
                break;
            default:
                break;
        }
        return color;
    }
```

4. Add an import into the `Estimote Beacon Manager-Prefix.pch` file:

   ```
   #import "LIBeaconHelper.h"
   ```

## Configuring the master view controller

Our master view controller just needs to tell us which beacons are nearby and allow our user to choose them. Consider the following steps:

1. Open `LIMasterViewController.h` and import the `ESTBeaconManager.h` class:

   ```
   #import <EstimoteSDK/ESTBeaconManager.h>
   ```

2. Add the `ESTBeaconManagerDelegate` protocol declaration to the `LIMasterViewController` declaration.

3. Add `ESTBeaconManager` as a property:

   ```
   @property (nonatomic, strong) ESTBeaconManager * beaconManager;
   ```

4. Our table view cell is going to present the beacon major and minor values and also the color of the beacon. For that, we need a better prototype cell type. Open `Main.storyboard`, locate the `MasterViewController` view, and change the prototype cell `Style` to `Left Detail`.

5. Open `LIMasterViewController.m`, and in the private interface declaration, add a local property to hold the beacons:

   ```
   @property (nonatomic, strong) NSArray * beacons;
   ```

6. Clear out the `viewDidLoad` method; we don't need an add or edit button in our implementation.

*Chapter 7*

# Configuring our beacon manager

We're going to need to create our beacon manager and clear out any existing beacon manager if it already exists. Consider the following steps:

1. Just after the call to `[super viewWillAppear:animated]`, add our call to clear out and recreate our beacon manager:

   ```
   if (self.beaconManager) {
       [self.beaconManager stopEstimoteBeaconDiscovery];
   }
   self.beaconManager = [[ESTBeaconManager alloc] init];
   ```

2. Next, we need to tell our beacon manager to return all the beacons for different regions in one collection:

   ```
   self.beaconManager.returnAllRangedBeaconsAtOnce = YES;
   ```

3. Now, we need to set view controller as the `ESTBeaconManager` delegate and start discovering beacons. By passing `nil` to the `startEstimoteBeaconsDiscoveryForRegion:` method, we're asking the manager to bring back all nearby Estimote beacons:

   ```
   self.beaconManager.delegate = self;
   [self.beaconManager
     startEstimoteBeaconsDiscoveryForRegion:nil];
   ```

4. Our `beaconManager:didDiscoverBeacons:inRegion` method from the `ESTBeaconManagerDelegate` protocol needs to set the local beacons property and then reload the table data:

   ```
   -(void)beaconManager:(ESTBeaconManager *)manager
     didDiscoverBeacons:(NSArray *)beacons
     inRegion:(ESTBeaconRegion *)region {

       NSSortDescriptor *major = [NSSortDescriptor
         sortDescriptorWithKey:@"major" ascending:YES];
       NSSortDescriptor *minor = [NSSortDescriptor
         sortDescriptorWithKey:@"minor" ascending:YES];
       self.beacons = [beacons
         sortedArrayUsingDescriptors:@[major, minor]];
       [self.tableView reloadData];
   }
   ```

5. Finally, `tableView:cellForRowAtIndexPath:` needs to return the table cell for our beacon. Replace the existing method with our own method:

   ```
   - (UITableViewCell *)tableView:(UITableView *)tableView
     cellForRowAtIndexPath:(NSIndexPath *)indexPath
   {
   ```

```
        UITableViewCell *cell = [tableView
          dequeueReusableCellWithIdentifier:@"Cell"
          forIndexPath:indexPath];

        ESTBeacon * beacon = [self.beacons
          objectAtIndex:indexPath.row];

        cell.detailTextLabel.text = [LIBeaconHelper
          colorNameForBeacon:beacon];
        cell.textLabel.text = [NSString
          stringWithFormat:@"%@:%@", beacon.major,
          beacon.minor];
        return cell;
}
```

## Configuring the detail view controller

The detail view controller needs to connect to the selected beacon before showing the details of the beacon and allowing the details to be changed. Consider the following steps for configuring the detail view controller:

1. Start by adding the Estimote SDK and Audio Toolbox imports to `LIDetailViewController.h`:

   ```
   #import <EstimoteSDK/ESTBeacon.h>
   #import <AudioToolbox/AudioToolbox.h>
   ```

2. Our view controller needs to act as the beacon delegate. Add the `ESTBeaconDelegate` declaration to the class declaration.

3. Next, we're going to need three text fields: a status label, a save button, and an activity indicator. Add the properties to the header file:

   ```
   @property (weak, nonatomic) IBOutlet UITextField
   *proximityUUIDTextField;
   @property (weak, nonatomic) IBOutlet UITextField *majorTextField;
   @property (weak, nonatomic) IBOutlet UITextField *minorTextField;
   @property (weak, nonatomic) IBOutlet UILabel *statusLabel;
   @property (weak, nonatomic) IBOutlet UIButton *saveButton;
   @property (weak, nonatomic) IBOutlet UIActivityIndicatorView
   *activityIndicator;
   ```

## Chapter 7

# Configuring the view

When the beacon instance is passed to our view controller, we need to determine its the state before disabling/enabling the save button, and then we attempt connecting to the beacon if it isn't connected already.

Consider the following steps for configuring the view:

1. Replace the implementation of `setDetailItem:` with this one:

    ```
    - (void)setDetailItem:(id)newDetailItem
    {
        if (_detailItem != newDetailItem) {
            _detailItem = newDetailItem;

            ESTBeacon * beacon = (ESTBeacon*)_detailItem;

            beacon.delegate = self;
            if (beacon.peripheral.state == CBPeripheralStateConnected)
    {
                [self.saveButton setEnabled:YES];
                [self.activityIndicator stopAnimating];
            }
            else {
                [self.saveButton setEnabled:NO];
                [((ESTBeacon*)_detailItem) connect];
                [self.activityIndicator startAnimating];
            }


            // Update the view.
            [self configureView];
        }
    }
    ```

2. We also need to update the `configureView` method based on the current connection status. Replace the implementation with our own implementation, which enables the save button only when the connection is made and sets the control values from the beacon:

    ```
    - (void)configureView
    {
        // Update the user interface for the detail item.
        ESTBeacon * beacon = (ESTBeacon*)self.detailItem;

        switch (beacon.peripheral.state) {
            case CBPeripheralStateConnected:
                self.statusLabel.text = @"Connected";
    ```

[ 139 ]

```
            [self.saveButton setEnabled:YES];
            break;
        default:
            self.title = @"Connecting...";
            self.statusLabel.text = @"Connecting...";
            [self.saveButton setEnabled:NO];
            break;
    }

    self.majorTextField.text = [beacon.major stringValue];
    self.minorTextField.text = [beacon.minor stringValue];
    self.proximityUUIDTextField.text = [beacon.proximityUUID UUIDString];
}
```

## Connecting and disconnecting from beacons

We're going to implement three `ESTBeaconDelegate` methods that handle when the beacon connects, when the beacon disconnects, and when the accelerometer values have changed. Consider the following steps for connecting and disconnecting from beacons:

1. Let's start with the `beaconConnectionDidSucceeded:` method. Here, we'll enable the accelerometer and set the title of our view controller using the temperature values from the beacon. We'll also enable the save button:

    ```
    -(void)beaconConnectionDidSucceeded:(ESTBeacon *)beacon {

        [self.navigationItem setRightBarButtonItem:nil];
        NSLog(@"Connected to beacon %@", beacon);

        [beacon enableAccelerometer:YES completion:nil];

        [self configureView];

        self.statusLabel.text = @"Connected";

        [beacon readTemperatureWithCompletion:^(NSNumber *value, NSError *error) {
            self.title = [NSString stringWithFormat:@"%@ - %@°C", [LIBeaconHelper colorNameForBeacon:beacon], value];
        }];

        [self.saveButton setEnabled:YES];
        [self.activityIndicator stopAnimating];
    }
    ```

*Chapter 7*

2. Next, we'll implement the `beaconConnectionDidFail:withError:` method. This method might occur multiple times with transient errors, which we can ignore. If a permanent error occurs, then we pop the view controller off the navigation stack; the user can try again if this occurs. Add the implementation:

   ```
   -(void)beaconConnectionDidFail:(ESTBeacon *)beacon
   withError:(NSError *)error {
       NSLog(@"Failed to connect to beacon: %@", error);
       if (error.code == 404) [[self navigationController]
   popViewControllerAnimated:YES];
   }
   ```

3. Finally, we want the accelerometer to detail changes by vibrating our device when changes occur. Add the delegate method `beacon:accelerometer StateChanged:`:

   ```
   -(void)beacon:(ESTBeacon *)beacon accelerometerStateChanged:(BOOL)
   state {
       AudioServicesPlayAlertSound(kSystemSoundID_Vibrate);
   }
   ```

## Saving the changes

The main piece to our detail view controller is to save the changes to the beacon when the save button is pressed. When we save the values, we need to write them independently to the device using the `writeProximityUUID:completion:`, `writeMajor:completion:`, and `writeMinor:completion:` values sequentially.

In order to ensure the values are written successfully, we'll chain the calls to write the values in the completion block in the previous call.

In each call, we'll check the success of the call before making the next one; if the call fails, we'll show an error. Consider the following steps for saving the changes:

1. Add a method to show an error message and re-enable the `save` function if an error occurs:

   ```
   -(void)showErrorAndEnableSave:(NSError*)error {
       UIAlertView * av = [[UIAlertView alloc]
          initWithTitle:@"An error occurred"
       message:error.description
       delegate:nil
       cancelButtonTitle:@"Ok"
       otherButtonTitles:nil, nil];
       
       [av show];
   ```

[ 141 ]

# Vendor SDKs – Buying and Configuring Beacons

```
        [self.activityIndicator stopAnimating];
        [self.saveButton setEnabled:YES];
    }
```

2. Add our save method to set the values of the device:

```
- (IBAction)saveChanges:(id)sender {
    ESTBeacon * beacon = (ESTBeacon*)self.detailItem;

    [self.navigationItem setHidesBackButton:
      YES animated:YES];
    [self.activityIndicator startAnimating];

    [beacon writeProximityUUID:
      self.proximityUUIDTextField.text
      completion:^(NSString *value, NSError *error) {
        if (error && error.code != 411) {
            [self showErrorAndEnableSave:error];
        }
        else {
            [beacon writeMajor:[self.majorTextField.text
              intValue] completion:^(unsigned short value,
              NSError *error) {
                if (error && error.code != 411) {
                    [self showErrorAndEnableSave:error];
                }
                else {
                    [beacon writeMinor:
                      [self.minorTextField.text intValue]
                      completion:^(unsigned short value,
                      NSError *error) {
                        if (error && error.code != 411) {
                            [self
                            showErrorAndEnableSave:error];
                        }
                        else {
                            [self.navigationItem
                              setHidesBackButton:NO
                              animated:YES];
                            [self.activityIndicator
                              stopAnimating];
                            [[self navigationController]
                              popViewControllerAnimated:YES];
                        }
                    }];
                }
            }];
        }
    }];
}
```

*Chapter 7*

This is a complex method that's doing quite a lot; so, let's go through it in sections.

First, it disables the back button and shows an activity indicator so that the user can't leave the view while it's trying to update the beacon:

```
ESTBeacon * beacon = (ESTBeacon*)self.detailItem;
[self.navigationItem setHidesBackButton:YES animated:YES];
[self.activityIndicator startAnimating];
```

Next, the code tries to use the Estimote SDK to configure the device, and takes some time to do so. The completion block is fired upon completion or failure:

```
[beacon writeProximityUUID:self.proximityUUIDTextField.text
completion:...]
```

The completion block then first checks to see whether an error occurred, and if so, we enable the save button again, as follows:

```
if (error && error.code != 411) {
[self showErrorAndEnableSave:error];
}
else {...}
```

If all is well, then the `else` statement attempts to write the major value, which also has a completion block:

```
[beacon writeMajor:[self majorTextField.text intValue] com-pletion:...]
```

The completion block again checks whether there's an error, and if so, re-enables the save button:

```
if (error && error.code != 411) {
[self showErrorAndEnableSave:error];
}
else {...}
```

Finally, if everything was successful, the `else` statement configures the minor value following the same structure as the previous write attempts with the additional code to stop the animation and pop off the view controller from the stack:

```
[beacon writeMinor:[self.minorTextField.text intValue]
completion:^(unsigned short value, NSError *error) {
if (error && error.code != 411) {
[self showErrorAndEnableSave:error];
    }
   else {
[self.navigationItem setHidesBackButton:NO animated:YES];
[self.activityIndicator stopAnimating];
```

```
            [[self navigationController] popViewControllerAnimated:YES];
    }
}];
```

## Creating the view

Finally, to make everything work, we need to wire up our view to the view controller.

Open up `Main.storyboard` and drag controls onto the view so that it resembles the following figure:

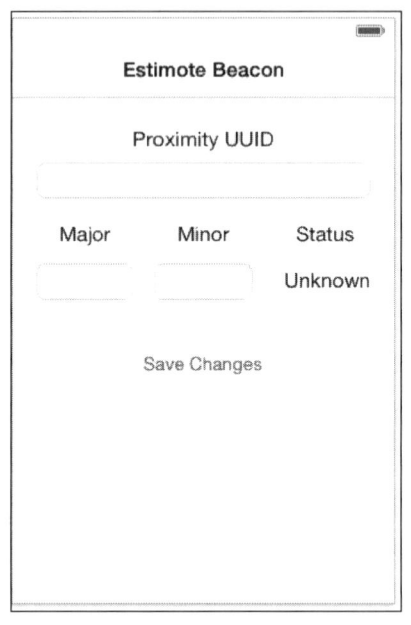

Our detail view

Ensure that you wire the following outlets to `LIDetailViewController.h`:

- `proximityUUIDTextField`
- `majorTextField`
- `minorTextField`
- `statusLabel`
- `saveButton`
- `activityIndicator`

Then, wire the `touchUpInside` event of the save button to `saveChanges: IBOutlet` in `LIDetailViewController.m`.

## Testing your application

Finally, you can fire up your application and get your Estimote beacons out.

Try changing some of your values and check whether it works. Don't forget to open a beacon in the detail view and then give the beacon a shake. Make sure it vibrates your iOS device!

## Summary

In this chapter, we explored the Estimote SDK in some detail as well as discussed some other vendor implementations of iBeacon.

In the next chapter, we will combine everything we've learned in the previous chapters to build a complete museum app.

# Advanced Tutorial – iBeacon Museum

So far throughout this book, you've learned about discovering beacons, determining the range of beacons, and even picking up and utilizing their presence when our app is running in the background. The aim of this chapter is to consolidate your knowledge into an app, which is as close to a real-world example as we can get.

In this chapter, we will not bring in any new iBeacon knowledge, but we will really get to grips with everything we learned throughout the book with an all-encompassing tutorial.

Our museum app allows users to wander around the exhibitions, and as they draw closer to the displays within each exhibition hall, they're given a more in-depth description of the context of what's on display.

Unlike in previous chapters, we will not use crude examples and try and mimic the kind of choices you'd make when considering user experience in a real-world app. A great example of this is that we'll ask for location permission by explaining to the user why we need location data and requesting them to click a button to grant permission before attempting to access the location information.

## Our exhibitions

Our iBeacon museum is made up of three exhibitions. Each exhibition contains three displays, which we'll refer to as exhibits.

Our entire museum will use the `1A285B28-EA1B-43F5-984A-CE5D2ED463CE` UUID. We'll be using major values to identify the exhibitions and the minor values to identify the exhibits beneath them as shown in the following figure:

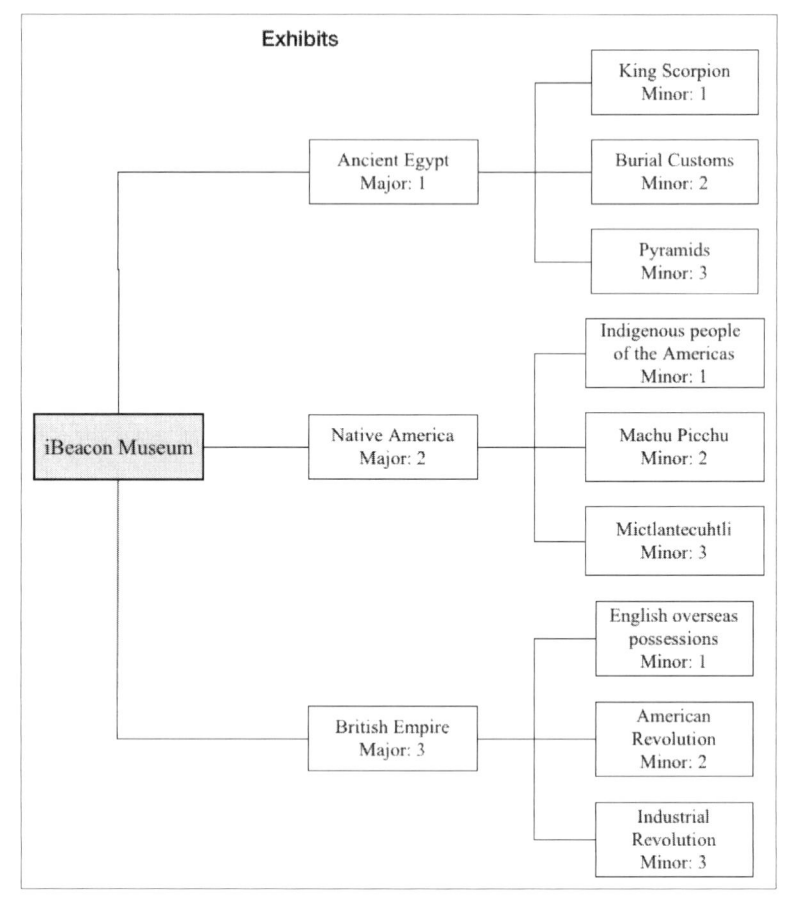

```
Exhibits
                                                    ┌─ King Scorpion    Minor: 1
                        ┌─ Ancient Egypt  Major: 1 ─┼─ Burial Customs   Minor: 2
                        │                           └─ Pyramids         Minor: 3
                        │
                        │                           ┌─ Indigenous people of the Americas  Minor: 1
iBeacon Museum ─────────┼─ Native America Major: 2 ─┼─ Machu Picchu     Minor: 2
                        │                           └─ Mictlantecuhtli  Minor: 3
                        │
                        │                           ┌─ English overseas possessions  Minor: 1
                        └─ British Empire  Major: 3 ┼─ American Revolution  Minor: 2
                                                    └─ Industrial Revolution Minor: 3
```

iBeacon museum exhibits

Because researching, collating, and even designing beautiful exhibit views is way beyond the scope of our app, what we'll be doing instead is using `UIWebView` to display our exhibit information. This way, we can concentrate on what's important for our app.

Other than skimming over the designs and using predefined, responsively-designed web views for our exhibit content, our app is pretty much a fully functioning real-world example. You can take the code base on this app and reuse it in a commercial application if you wish, and of course, you have my consent to do so. I'd love to see your commercial applications and will even feature them on this book's accompanying site `http://ibeacon.university/` if you let me know when they're published.

# The museum map

Our museum is made up of an atrium and three exhibition halls in a lovely hexagon design as shown in the following figure:

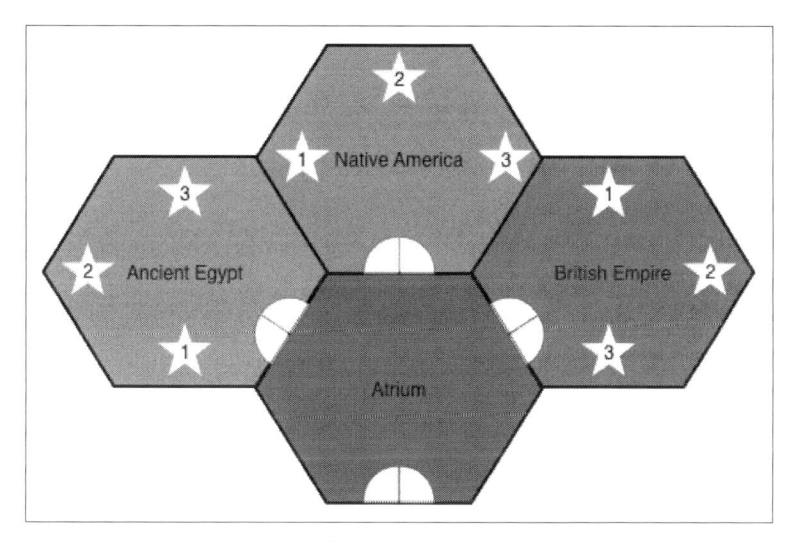

The museum map

The main entrance of our museum takes the visitor into the atrium. Once there, they can visit any of our three exhibitions, but always have to come back through the atrium. We'll assume that if the user isn't within 5 meters of any beacon, then they're probably in the atrium and we'll let them know what else they can visit in our museum.

# Our app structure

Our app is split into three views, which are automatically presented completely. There's no real navigation system to the application, the app navigation is controlled by where the user's feet take them.

# The permission view

The first view halts the users' access to the app until the app can determine that the location services are switched on for use by the app and that the user has given permission for the app to use their location.

Without location information, our app is useless, but rather than just assuming that we have it like we have in all of our other tutorials, we'll actually give users the reason why we need it and give them a much nicer user experience.

## The atrium view

The atrium view gives our user more information about the museum and a summary of the exhibits within. We'll be presenting the user with the atrium view when they're no closer than 5 meters to any exhibit beacon. When they're closer than that, we'll always present the user with an exhibit view.

The atrium view also has the responsibility for collecting the name of the users so that we can show them which exhibit they're closest to on the map.

## The exhibit view

Our final view shows contextual information about the exhibit that the user is nearest to. For example, if the user is right next to the industrial revolution exhibit of the British Empire exhibition, then the current view will be a cut-down version of the associated Wikipedia page about the industrial revolution of the British Empire.

This information view also contains a button that can be tapped and shows the user's location on the map rather than the current exhibit information.

If the user has already granted location permission, then we automatically jump to the museum view.

## The supporting website

In order to skip the design phase of this app and really concentrate on the iBeacon related functionality, I've provided the view and map content in a separate responsive website.

Most of the content of our app will be delivered as responsive web pages presented in `UIWebViews` from `http://museum.ibeacon.university/`.

Our companion site also uses real-time socket connections so that you can actually see which exhibit you're currently visiting in real time from any browser as shown in the following figure:

*Chapter 8*

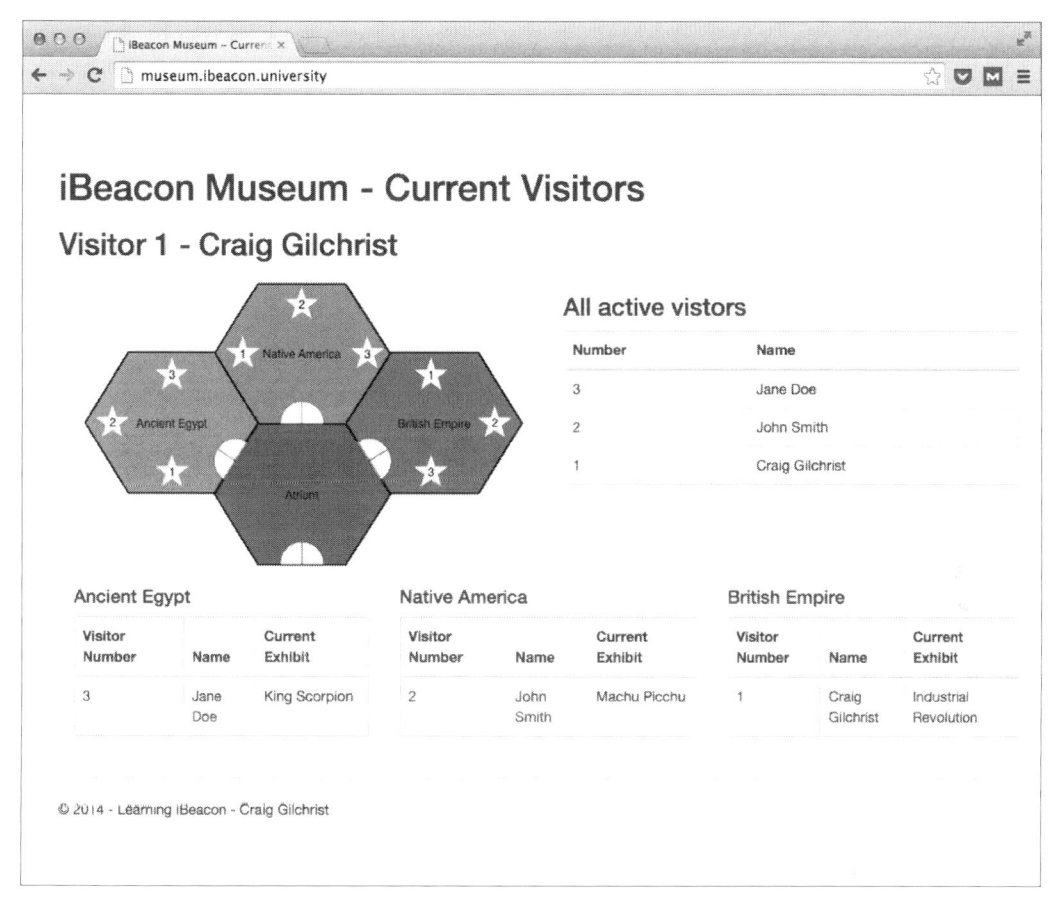

*iBeacon museum current visitors*

## Tracking our user's journey

The role of the supporting website is to track our user's journey but also to return the content associated to the beacon that they are nearest to. In order to do both and effectively track our user, we need to follow a strict order of calls to our service. We'll do this by maintaining a browser session in a hidden `UIWebView`, which belongs to our main view controller. Consider the following steps to track our user's journey:

1. Create `http://museum.ibeacon.university/name/{user_name}`, where {user_name} is replaced by the name of the visitor. This first call tells our server who our visitor is and also sets some cookies so that we can track our visitor's journey.

    For example, after entering my name, the URL would be `http://museum.ibeacon.university/name/Craig%20Gilchrist/`.

*Advanced Tutorial – iBeacon Museum*

2. For each exhibit, we then visit `http://museum.ibeacon.university/exhibit/{major}/{minor}`, where {major} and {minor} would be replaced by the major and minor values from the beacon. This URL then tracks the user's journey and then forwards the browser to the relevant Wikipedia page.

   For example, if we're closest to the Machu Picchu exhibit, our URL would be `http://museum.ibeacon.university/exhibit/2/2`.

3. Finally, we have a dedicated web page that returns our map for our overlay that shows where we are currently in the museum. The URL is similar to the exhibit URL with the exception that the exhibit path element has been replaced by a map path element: `http://museum.ibeacon.university/map/{major}/{minor}`.

## Our app design

Our app is going to be essentially a single view application with all of our functionalities being placed offscreen when it's not in use but still present within the view and ultimately owned by the view controller.

This is a nice and easy way to ensure that `UIWebView`, which is maintaining our session with the server, is always in memory, and so that we're not getting a new identity with the server every time, the view is released by our application.

The following figure gives a much clearer indication of how our app is designed:

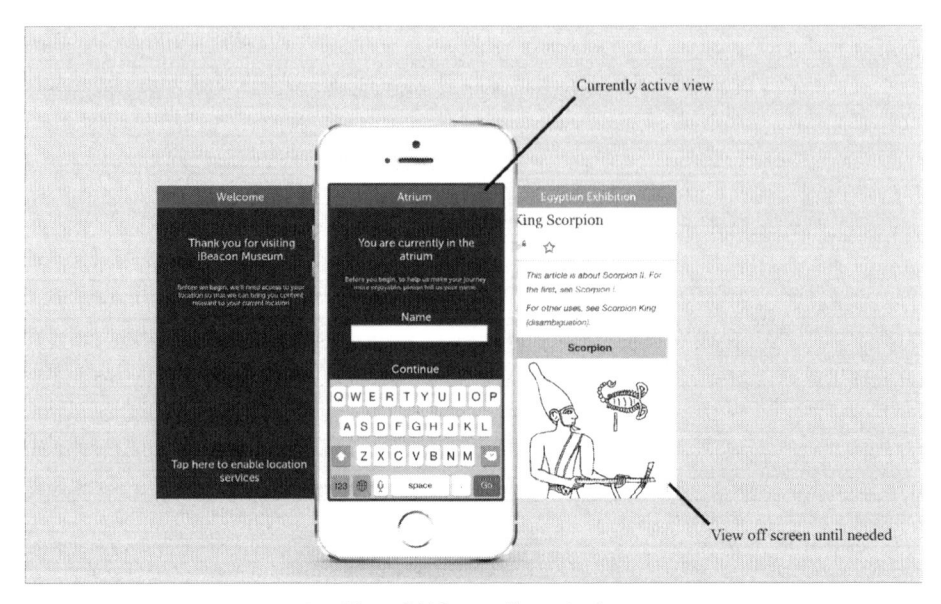

Views hidden until required

# Building the application

Now that we've fully explained our app and all of its features, let's build it!

## Creating the project

Follow these steps to create the project:

1. Start by firing up Xcode and choosing a single view application from the templates when prompted.
2. Enter the following options for your new project:
    - **Product Name**: `iBeacon Museum`
    - **Organization Name**: `Learning iBeacon`
    - **Product Identifier**: `com.learningibeacon`
    - **Devices**: `iPhone`
3. Before we begin coding, let's start by setting our project properties. Open up the project properties by clicking on the top-level project in **Project Navigator**, and then under **Deployment Info** ensure that you turn on the **Hide status bar** option. Also ensure that our iPhone app can only be displayed in portrait mode by ensuring that only **Portrait** is checked in the **Device Orientation** option.
4. We're going to be displaying a lot of Wikipedia content in our app so it makes sense to hide any other text when it's just content on the screen. Open the **Info** tab of our **Properties** window and under **Custom iOS Target Properties**, set the **View controller-based status bar appearance** property to **NO**. This will ensure that the status bar is never shown.
5. Under the **Linked Frameworks and Libraries** section in the **Info** tab, click on the add icon and add `CoreLocation.framework`.

## Initializing the views

We will not use nibs or storyboards for this tutorial. We'll be laying out each of the views in code (it is an *advanced* tutorial after all). We'll start by creating the views and positioning them offscreen first before building the functionality for each view. Perform the following steps to initialize the views:

1. Open our view controller implementation file. It will be named `ViewController.m` if you didn't choose a class prefix or `LIViewController.m` if you did as we did in the previous chapters.

*Advanced Tutorial – iBeacon Museum*

2. Add a property for each of our views in the implementation's interface section so that it resembles the following code:

   ```
   @interface ViewController ()

   @property (nonatomic, retain) UIView *
     locationPermissionView;
   @property (nonatomic, retain) UIView * exhibitView;
   @property (nonatomic, retain) UIView * atriumView;

   @end
   ```

3. Now, we need to instantiate our views. We'll be using our view controller's view frame to instantiate the views with frames and we'll offset the views we don't want to show to be just off the right-hand side of the view by setting the x-origin to be that of the view width. We'll also set the backgrounds for our atrium and permission views to a nice dark color. Add the following code:

   ```
   CGRect frame = self.view.frame;

       self.locationPermissionView = [[UIView alloc]
         initWithFrame:frame];

       // Set the frame off screen to the right.
       frame.origin.x = frame.size.width;

       self.exhibitView = [[UIView alloc] initWithFrame:frame];
       self.atriumView = [[UIView alloc] initWithFrame:frame];

       self.locationPermissionView.backgroundColor = [UIColor
         colorWithRed:37.f/255.f green:33.f/255.f
         blue:28.f/255.f alpha:1.f];
       self.atriumView.backgroundColor = self.
         locationPermissionView.backgroundColor;
   ```

Notice that we didn't add the views as subviews yet? That's because we're not entirely sure whether we should be presenting the permissions view or the atrium view since we don't know whether the user has already allowed access to their location.

# Adding the CoreLocation functionality

In order to determine whether we've been given permission to use the user's location, we need a `CLLocationManager` instance. Perform the following steps:

1. Switch over to your view controller header file and add an import declaration for `CoreLocation` and declare our view controller as a `CLLocationManager` delegate. Your header file contents should now look something like the following code implementation:

    ```
    #import <UIKit/UIKit.h>
    #import <CoreLocation/CoreLocation.h>

    @interface ViewController : UIViewController<CLLocationManagerDele
    gate>

    @end
    ```

2. Switch back to your implementation file and add a new `CLLocationManager` delegate and region properties:

    ```
    @property (nonatomic, retain) CLLocationManager *
      locationManager;
    @property (nonatomic, retain) CLBeaconRegion * region;
    ```

3. Just below where we set our atrium view background color, add a few lines to instantiate our location manager, set our view controller as the delegate, and create our beacon region:

    ```
    self.locationManager = [[CLLocationManager alloc] init];
    self.locationManager.delegate = self;
    NSUUID * beaconUUID = [[NSUUID alloc]
      initWithUUIDString:@"1A285B28-EA1B-43F5-984A-
      CE5D2ED463CE"];
    self.region = [[CLBeaconRegion alloc]
      initWithProximityUUID:beaconUUID identifier:@"Exhibits"];
    ```

# Determining the first view

Now that we can determine permission status, we can see whether or not to initially show the permission view or the atrium view. If `[CLLocationManager authorizationStatus]` reports a status of `kCLAuthorizationStatusAuthorized`, then we need to show the atrium view instead of the permission view.

Since our frame is already set to offscreen, we set our location permission view frame to that of our frame before resetting the x-origin back to zero and using it to reposition the atrium view. Perform the following steps:

1. Add this code just below the location manager instantiation code:

   ```
   CLAuthorizationStatus authStatus = [CLLocationManager
     authorizationStatus];

   if (authStatus == kCLAuthorizationStatusAuthorized) {
       self.locationPermissionView.frame = frame;
       frame.origin.x = 0;
       self.atriumView.frame = frame;
   }

   [self.view addSubview:self.exhibitView];
   [self.view addSubview:self.atriumView];
   [self.view addSubview:self.locationPermissionView];
   ```

2. In order to keep our code tidy, we'll configure the rest of the view details in the `viewDidAppear` method and call out to separate methods to configure each view independently. Add three method stubs to configure the view and a call to each in the `viewDidAppear` method:

   ```
   -(void)viewDidAppear:(BOOL)animated {
       [self configureAtriumView];
       [self configureExhibitView];
       [self configurePermissionView];
   }

   -(void)configureAtriumView {

   }

   -(void)configurePermissionView {

   }

   -(void)configureExhibitView {

   }
   ```

[ 156 ]

## Configuring our permission view

Now that we've created a method stub to configure our permission view, we can go ahead and add the pieces we need. We'll add another check to `CLLocationManager` to see whether the user has actually denied location services and show a message if they have; otherwise, we'll add a button to ask for the permission.

Let's start by wiring up our `CLLocationManager` delegate method, `locationManager:didChangeAuthorizationStatus` so that it shows an error message if the user has denied location authorization. First, we'll need a method that checks and sets the label and button properties of our view depending on the authorization status. Consider the following steps:

1. Add the following method:

    ```
    -(void)setPermissionInstructions {
    
        UILabel * permissionInstructions =
          (UILabel*)[self.locationPermissionView
          viewWithTag:1];
        UIButton * permissionButton =
        (UIButton*)[self.locationPermissionView viewWithTag:2];
    
        if ([CLLocationManager authorizationStatus] ==
          kCLAuthorizationStatusDenied) {
            [permissionInstructions setText:@"Allow permissions
              in the system preferences under Privacy >
              Location Services > iBeacon Museum"];
            [permissionButton setHidden:YES];
        }
        else {
            [permissionInstructions setText:@"Before we begin,
              we'll need access to your location so that we can
              bring you content relevant to your current
              location"];
            [permissionButton setHidden:NO];
        }
    }
    ```

2. Now, we can add our `locationManager:didChangeAuthorizationStatus:` method to hide the welcome view if the user grants permission or changes the instructions if they don't grant permission:

    ```
    -(void)locationManager:(CLLocationManager *)manager
      didChangeAuthorizationStatus:
      (CLAuthorizationStatus)status {
    
        [self setPermissionInstructions];
    ```

*Advanced Tutorial – iBeacon Museum*

```objc
    if (status == kCLAuthorizationStatusAuthorized) {
        // Animate in the atrium view.
        CGRect frame = self.view.frame;
        CGRect offsetLeftFrame = CGRectMake(-
            frame.size.width, 0, frame.size.width,
            frame.size.height);

        [UIView animateWithDuration:0.5f animations:^{
            self.locationPermissionView.frame =
                offsetLeftFrame;
            self.atriumView.frame = frame;
        }];
    }
}
```

3. We'll also need a method to start monitoring our beacon region. Add the method now:

```objc
-(void)startMonitoringForRegion {
    NSUUID * beaconUUID = [[NSUUID alloc]
        initWithUUIDString:@"1A285B28-EA1B-43F5-
        984A-CE5D2ED463CE"];
    CLBeaconRegion * region = [[CLBeaconRegion alloc]
        initWithProximityUUID:beaconUUID
        identifier:@"Exhibits"];
    [self.locationManager startMonitoringForRegion:region];
}
```

## Adding controls

Now, finally we need to create all of the controls for our view. Notice, that we retrieved the labels and views using their tags in the setPermissionInstructions method so we'll need to make sure we add tags. This method is quite large, so I'll break it down into sections. Perform the following steps:

1. First, we need to create UINavigationBar to section off our page nicely. Add the following code to the configurePermissionView method:

```objc
UINavigationBar * navbar = [[UINavigationBar alloc]
    init];
navbar.barTintColor = [UIColor colorWithRed:129.f/255.
    f green:76.f/255.f blue:166.f/255.f alpha:1.f];
navbar.translucent = NO;
[navbar setFrame:CGRectMake(0, 0,
    self.locationPermissionView.frame.size.width, 44.f)];
[self.locationPermissionView addSubview:navbar];
```

*Chapter 8*

2. Now, add a title label to the navbar:

   ```
   UILabel * titleLabel = [[UILabel alloc]
     initWithFrame:navbar.frame];
   [titleLabel setText:@"Welcome"];
   [titleLabel setTextAlignment:NSTextAlignmentCenter];
   [titleLabel setTextColor:[UIColor whiteColor]];
   [navbar addSubview:titleLabel];
   ```

3. We'll use the navbar height to position our next welcome label:

   ```
   UILabel * welcomeLabel = [[UILabel alloc] initWithFrame:
   CGRectMake(10.f, titleLabel.frame.size.height + 10.f,
     self.view.frame.size.width-20.f, 60.f)];
   [welcomeLabel setTextColor:[UIColor whiteColor]];
   [welcomeLabel setTextAlignment:NSTextAlignmentCenter];
   [welcomeLabel setText:@"Thank you for visiting iBeacon
     Museum."];
   [welcomeLabel setFont:[UIFont systemFontOfSize:20.f]];
   [welcomeLabel setNumberOfLines:0];
   [self.locationPermissionView addSubview:welcomeLabel];
   ```

4. Now, we'll give a tag value of 1 to all our important instruction's label and use the welcome label to position it:

   ```
   UILabel * instructionsLabel = [[UILabel alloc]
     initWithFrame:
   CGRectMake(10.f, welcomeLabel.frame.origin.y +
     welcomeLabel.frame.size.height + 20.f,
     self.view.frame.size.width-20.f, 120.f)];
   [instructionsLabel setTextColor:[UIColor whiteColor]];
   [instructionsLabel setTextAlignment:NSTextAlignmentCenter];
   [instructionsLabel setTag:1];
   instructionsLabel.numberOfLines = 0;
   [self.locationPermissionView addSubview:instructionsLabel];
   ```

5. Now, we need to add a button to start region monitoring which will request permission the first time the user presses it. We need to grab this button in the setPermissionInstructions method so we need to give it a tag of 2:

   ```
   UIButton * button = [[UIButton alloc] initWithFrame:
     CGRectMake(10, self.view.frame.size.height-54.f,
     self.view.frame.size.width-20.f, 44.f)];
   [button setTag:2];
   [button setTitle:@"Tap to allow location"
     forState:UIControlStateNormal];
   [button addTarget:self
     action:@selector(startMonitoringForRegion)
     forControlEvents:UIControlEventTouchUpInside];
   [self.locationPermissionView addSubview:button];
   ```

6. Finally, we need to set the permission instruction properties for our newly added labels and buttons, as follows:

   ```
   [self setPermissionInstructions];
   ```

## Configuring the exhibit view

Our exhibit view's responsibility is to load the web content corresponding to the nearest beacon. If there isn't a beacon near, then we show the atrium view.

Our exhibit view is also responsible for sending our users name up to the server. Let's start by creating our web view. It contains a simple navigation bar and a web view filling the rest of the page. Inside our navigation bar, we also got a button that switches between map mode and detail mode. Perform the following steps:

1. We'll keep the important fields as properties so that we don't have to keep hunting them down from the sub views. Add the following properties to our view controller:

   ```
   @property (nonatomic, retain) UILabel * exhibitLabel;
   @property (nonatomic) BOOL isMapMode;
   @property (nonatomic) BOOL hasSentNameToServer;
   @property (nonatomic, retain) UINavigationBar *
     exhibitNavbar;
   @property (nonatomic, retain) UIWebView * mapWebView;
   @property (nonatomic, retain) UIWebView * detailWebView;
   ```

2. Add a method to switch between the map and detail mode. This method simply needs to set the local `isMapMode` property and hide one or more of the web views:

   ```
   -(void)switchMapMode {
       self.isMapMode = !self.isMapMode;
       self.mapWebView.hidden = !self.isMapMode;
       self.detailWebView.hidden = self.isMapMode;
   }
   ```

3. Our app needs to know when it can switch over to the exhibit view, and it can only do this once the name has been sent to the server. Add the `UIWebViewDelegate` declaration to our controller header file and then add the following method so that we know that our app can start showing exhibits as soon as they come into range:

   ```
   -(void)webViewDidFinishLoad:(UIWebView *)webView {
       self.detailWebView.delegate = nil;

       self.hasSentNameToServer = YES;
   ```

```
      UILabel * atriumInstructions =
        (UILabel*)[self.atriumView viewWithTag:2];
      [atriumInstructions setText:@"As you browse the museum
        we'll present information relevant to you"];

      [self startMonitoringForRegion];
    }
```

4. Now, be sure to make our controller the delegate of the web view at the end of the `configureExhibitView` method:

   ```
   self.detailWebView.delegate = self;
   ```

## Adding controls to the exhibit view

Now, we need to add our controls to the exhibit view. It's very straightforward but again, there's a lot of code so we'll do it in sections. Perform the following steps:

1. Just like the permission view, we need a navigation bar; although this time, we keep a reference in our controller property. Add the following code to our `configureExhibitView` method:

   ```
   UINavigationBar * navbar = [[UINavigationBar alloc] init];
       navbar.barTintColor = [UIColor colorWithRed:129.f/255.f
         green:76.f/255.f blue:166.f/255.f alpha:1.f];
       navbar.translucent = NO;
       [navbar setFrame:CGRectMake(0, 0,
         self.locationPermissionView.frame.size.width, 44.f)];
       [self.exhibitView addSubview:navbar];
       self.exhibitNavbar = navbar;
   ```

2. Now, add a title and keep a reference in our property:

   ```
   UILabel * titleLabel = [[UILabel alloc]
     initWithFrame:navbar.frame];
   [titleLabel setText:@"Exhibit"];
   [titleLabel setTextAlignment:NSTextAlignmentCenter];
   [titleLabel setTextColor:[UIColor whiteColor]];
   [navbar addSubview:titleLabel];
   self.exhibitLabel = titleLabel;
   ```

3. Add a navigation item with a right bar button item to switch our view from the info to map views:

   ```
   UIButton * button = [UIButton
     buttonWithType:UIButtonTypeDetailDisclosure];
       CGRect frame = button.frame;
       frame.origin.x = navbar.frame.size.width - 10.0f -
         frame.size.width;
   ```

## Advanced Tutorial – iBeacon Museum

```
    frame.origin.y = (navbar.frame.size.height/2)-
      (frame.size.height/2);
    button.tintColor = [UIColor whiteColor];
    [button addTarget:self action:@selector(switchMapMode)
      forControlEvents:UIControlEventTouchUpInside];
    [button setFrame:frame];
    [navbar addSubview:button];
```

4. Now, add our web views and again keep a local reference:

```
    UIWebView * detailWebView = [[UIWebView alloc]
      initWithFrame:CGRectMake(0, navbar.frame.size.height, self.view.
    frame.size.width, self.view.frame.size.height-
    navbar.frame.size.height)];
    UIWebView * mapWebView = [[UIWebView alloc]
    initWithFrame:detailWebView.frame];
    [mapWebView setHidden:YES];
    self.detailWebView = detailWebView;
    self.mapWebView = mapWebView;
    [self.exhibitView addSubview:detailWebView];
    [self.exhibitView addSubview:mapWebView];
```

## Adding content methods

To complete our exhibit view, we need two methods, one to show content and another to set the name. Perform the following steps:

1. Add the method to send the user's name to the server. We'll be using the `UITextField` value from the atrium view, which we'll create shortly.

2. This method grabs the text field and forms the URL using its text value before sending the value and then starts monitoring for location:

```
    -(void)sendNameToServer {
        UITextField * nameTextField = (UITextField*)[self.atriumView
    viewWithTag:1];
        NSString * urlString = [NSString stringWithFormat:@"http://
    museum.ibeacon.university/name/%@", [nameTextField.text stringByAd
    dingPercentEscapesUsingEncoding:NSASCIIStringEncoding]];
        [self.detailWebView loadRequest:[NSURLRequest
    requestWithURL:[NSURL URLWithString:urlString]]];
        [self startMonitoringForRegion];
    }
```

# Ranging beacons

The last things we need to do to finish our exhibit view is range beacons and show the relevant details. Perform the following steps:

1. First, add major and minor properties so that we know what our current view exhibit is:

   ```
   @property (nonatomic) int currentMajor;
   @property (nonatomic) int currentMinor;
   ```

2. Now, add our `locationManager:didRangeBeacons:inRegion` method stub:

   ```
   -(void)locationManager:(CLLocationManager *)manager
     didRangeBeacons:(NSArray *)beacons
     inRegion:(CLBeaconRegion *)region
   {
   }
   ```

3. To our new method stub, add the following code that prepares some frames for the relevant views and determines which is the closest beacon:

   ```
   if (!self.hasSentNameToServer) return;
   CGRect frame = self.view.frame;
       CGRect offsetLeftFrame = CGRectMake(-frame.size.width,
         0, frame.size.width, frame.size.height);

       CLBeacon * closestBeacon = nil;
       for (CLBeacon * beacon in beacons) {
           if (closestBeacon == nil) {
               closestBeacon = beacon;
           }
           else {
               if (beacon.accuracy < closestBeacon.accuracy) {
                   closestBeacon = beacon;
               }
           }
       }
   ```

4. Now, we need to determine whether we have a beacon within 5 meters and if so, we need to show the exhibit view by loading the content into our web views and ensuring the atrium view isn't being shown:

   ```
   if (closestBeacon && closestBeacon.accuracy < 5) {
       self.atriumView.frame = offsetLeftFrame;
       self.exhibitView.frame = frame;

       if (self.currentMajor != [closestBeacon.major
         intValue] || self.currentMinor !=
         [closestBeacon.minor intValue]) {
   ```

## Advanced Tutorial – iBeacon Museum

```objc
            self.currentMajor =[closestBeacon.major
              intValue];
            self.currentMinor =[closestBeacon.minor
              intValue];

            NSURL * detailUrl = [NSURL
              URLWithString:[NSString
              stringWithFormat:@
              "http://museum.ibeacon.university/exhibit
              /%i/%i", self.currentMajor, self.currentMinor]];
                NSURL * mapUrl = [NSURL URLWithString:[NSString
                    stringWithFormat:@"http://museum.ibeacon.
                    university/map/%i/%i", self.currentMajor,
                    self.currentMinor]];

                [self.detailWebView loadRequest:[NSURLRequest
                    requestWithURL:detailUrl]];
                [self.mapWebView loadRequest:[NSURLRequest
                    requestWithURL:mapUrl]];
            }
        }
        if (self.currentMajor == 1) {
            self.exhibitNavbar.barTintColor = [UIColor
              colorWithRed:95.f/255.f green:185.f/255.f
              blue:89.f/255.f alpha:1.f];
            self.exhibitLabel.text = @"Ancient Egypt";
        }
        if (self.currentMajor == 2) {
            self.exhibitNavbar.barTintColor = [UIColor
              colorWithRed:85.f/255.f green:159.f/255.f
              blue:208.f/255.f alpha:1.f];
            self.exhibitLabel.text = @"Native America";
        }
        if (self.currentMajor == 3) {
            self.exhibitNavbar.barTintColor = [UIColor
              coloWithRed:188.f/255.f green:88.f/255.f
              blue:88.f/255.f alpha:1.f];
            self.exhibitLabel.text = @"British Empire";
        }
```

5. If we don't have a beacon nearby, then we should show the atrium view. Add an `else if` statement as follows:

```objc
else if (self.currentMajor > 0) {
    self.exhibitView.frame = offsetLeftFrame;
    self.atriumView.frame = frame;
    self.currentMajor = 0;
    self.currentMinor = 0;
};
```

*Chapter 8*

# Configuring our atrium view

Our final view is the atrium view, which is a holding view for when there are no beacons within 5 meters, or we've not yet got the user's name. It makes sense then that the first thing we need to do is collect the user's name. Perform the following steps:

1. Jump back over to our `ViewController` header file and declare the controller `UITextFieldDelegate`.

   Once we've got an acceptable answer for a name, we need to hide the text field and make our first web call to the server, which we already configured. In order to know when we should start monitoring beacons, we need to use the `textFieldShouldReturn:` method of `UITextFieldDelegate`. Once we've got an acceptable value, we'll call our `sendNameToServer` method we created earlier.

2. Now, add the following code to ensure the text field isn't empty:

   ```
   -(BOOL)textFieldShouldReturn:(UITextField *)textField {
       if ([textField.text stringByTrimmingCharactersInSet:[NSCharacterSet whitespaceAndNewlineCharacterSet]]) {
           [textField setHidden:YES];
           [textField resignFirstResponder];
           [self sendNameToServer];
           return YES;
       }
       return NO;
   }
   ```

## Adding atrium view controls

The last thing to do before testing our app is to configure the atrium view controls. This doesn't need any detailed explanation as it's very similar to the other control creation methods, except to note that we're using a tag value of 1 for the text field and a tag value of 2 for the instructions as we need to grab these in other methods we've created earlier.

Complete `configureAtriumView` so that it looks like the following snippet:

```
-(void)configureAtriumView {
    UINavigationBar * navbar = [[UINavigationBar alloc] init];
    navbar.barTintColor = [UIColor colorWithRed:129.f/255.f
      green:76.f/255.f blue:166.f/255.f alpha:1.f];
    navbar.translucent = NO;
    [navbar setFrame:CGRectMake(0, 0,
      self.atriumView.frame.size.width, 44.f)];
    [self.atriumView addSubview:navbar];
```

[ 165 ]

```objc
    // Add a title.
    UILabel * titleLabel = [[UILabel alloc]
      initWithFrame:navbar.frame];
    [titleLabel setText:@"Atrium"];
    [titleLabel setTextAlignment:NSTextAlignmentCenter];
    [titleLabel setTextColor:[UIColor whiteColor]];
    [navbar addSubview:titleLabel];

    // Add instructions and labels.
    UILabel * welcomeLabel = [[UILabel alloc] initWithFrame:
      CGRectMake(10.f,
      titleLabel.frame.size.height + 10.f,
      self.view.frame.size.width-20.f,
      60.f)];
    [welcomeLabel setTextColor:[UIColor whiteColor]];
    [welcomeLabel setTextAlignment:NSTextAlignmentCenter];
    [welcomeLabel setText:@"You are currently in the atrium"];
    [welcomeLabel setFont:[UIFont systemFontOfSize:20.f]];
    [welcomeLabel setNumberOfLines:0];
    [self.atriumView addSubview:welcomeLabel];

    UILabel * instructionsLabel = [[UILabel alloc] initWithFrame:
        CGRectMake(10.f,
        welcomeLabel.frame.origin.y +
          welcomeLabel.frame.size.height + 20.f,
        self.view.frame.size.width-20.f,
        80.f)];
    [instructionsLabel setTextColor:[UIColor whiteColor]];
    [instructionsLabel setTextAlignment:NSTextAlignmentCenter];
    instructionsLabel.numberOfLines = 0;
    [instructionsLabel setText:@"Before you begin, to help us make
      your journey more enjoyable, please tell us your name."];
    instructionsLabel.tag = 2;
    [self.atriumView addSubview:instructionsLabel];

    UITextField * textField = [[UITextField alloc]
      initWithFrame:CGRectMake(10.f,
      instructionsLabel.frame.origin.y +
      instructionsLabel.frame.size.height + 10.f,
      self.view.frame.size.width-20.f, 44.f)];
    [textField setDelegate:self];
    textField.tag = 1;
    textField.backgroundColor = [UIColor whiteColor];
    [textField setReturnKeyType:UIReturnKeyGo];
    [self.atriumView addSubview:textField];
}
```

There's quite a lot of code in this snippet, but most of it is just layout and styling code. What the code does in a sequential order is:

1. Configures the navigation bar.
2. Adds a title label.
3. Adds a welcome label just below the title.
4. Creates `UITextField`, sets the current ViewController as the delegate, and then adds it to the view.

## Time to test

This really has been a *huge* tutorial and so there's a good chance that you might have missed a step. If something doesn't work quite like you expected it to, then go through each step again and download the completed source code from the companion site to compare it with your own to see what you might have missed.

Use the companion OS X app to act as your beacons and don't forget to open a separate browser window for `http://museum.ibeacon.university/` to see your progress (as well as others) on the web too.

Finally, feel free to amend, adapt, and refactor any of the code or feel free to catch me on Twitter if you have any questions about this tutorial (`@craiggilchrist`).

## Summary

This chapter really was just to reinforce everything you've learned throughout this book. The final chapter looks at some security issues surrounding iBeacon and also what the future holds for the technology.

As far as coding goes, this was the final tutorial in the book. I hope you've really got to grips with the amazing potential of this technology and you are well armed with all the coding skills you need to build amazing proximity-powered applications.

In the next chapter, we'll discuss some of the security aspects of deploying iBeacon solutions including spoofing, hacking, and overcoming user fears with good user experience.

# 9
# iBeacon Security – Understanding the Risks

The final chapter of this book is about understanding the security issues surrounding iBeacon for you as both a developer and a consumer. If you've followed all of the tutorials in this book, then you've already got a good understanding of what security issues you might face as a developer. This chapter gives more depth to that understanding.

I thought a rundown of some security considerations together with a vocabulary of common security concerns of users would be a great way to finish off the book.

We've covered some of the security risks in *Chapter 1*, *Welcome to iBeacon*, so we may go over some old ground but since this chapter is entirely dedicated to security, we'll cover the topics in more depth.

## Beacon spoofing

As a developer, one of your primary concerns should be the vulnerability of your iBeacon profile. It's very easy for anyone equipped with a Bluetooth sniffer app to determine your beacon signatures and spoof them in their own app. After all, you've already made your iPhone act as a beacon during the course of this book.

The **Consumer Electronics Show (CES)** 2014 offered its visitors a treasure hunt powered by iBeacons and before the conference even began, the show had been hacked by the team at Make Magazine so that they could win the treasure hunt without even being at the event. Read more about Make's audacious hack at `http://bit.ly/makehacks`.

What Make Magazine did is downloaded the Android APK file (a compiled zip containing the Android app) and ran it through a decompiler to discover the beacon profiles used by CES.

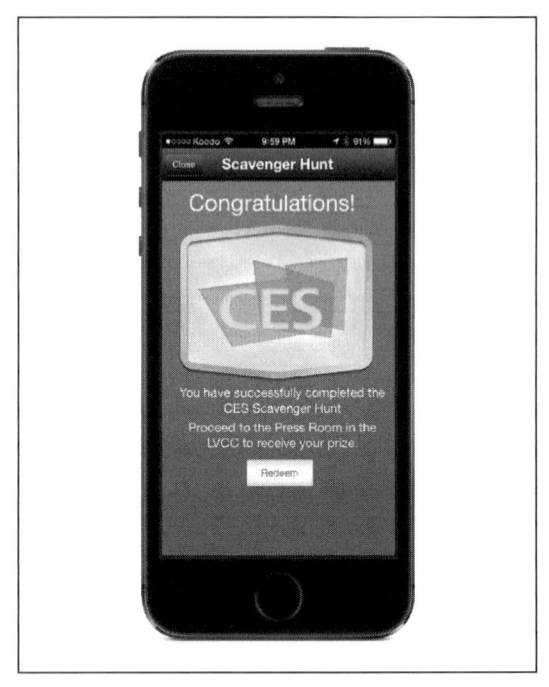

CES treasure hunt winner

## Defending against beacon spoofing

Ultimately, the best way to defend against people maliciously is to first decide whether or not you care?

If your beacon profile is used to send marketing messages or some benign functionality, then it's safe to opt for a very low level security mechanism. If you decide that the assets that the beacon represents are more valuable and the functionality needs protecting, then it's time to face the facts. Your beacon profile can be hacked and discovered easily and so, your app needs to employ extra clues to determine whether your device really is within the range of the beacon.

You can use other cues to determine whether this is actually your beacon, such as GPS location, or user behavior (has the user passed other beacons that you know are nearby?).

Another way of managing your beacon security is by actually delivering the beacon profiles to your app using a web service via a content management system. This way, when one gets spoofed, you can easily stop monitoring it.

## Rotating UUIDs

Gimbal beacons use a rotating UUID in which you use an SDK that queries a secure web API to give you the UUID of the beacons. The beacons are also smart and change the UUID without any internet connectivity.

This is a fantastic way of securing beacon deployments, as once deployed, the beacons are essentially useless without using the API. There is however a significant cost involved to using Gimbal as your solution provider as the SDK and cloud platform is charged on a *per user* basis.

## Beacon hacking

We've already discussed buying beacons and different types of beacons in *Chapter 1, Welcome to iBeacon* and *Chapter 7, Vendor SDKs – Buying and Configuring Beacons*, so we already know that there are various differences in the way beacon vendors implement their security models.

Beacon vendors have a catch-22 situation. They need a way to allow you as the owner to configure the UUID, major, and minor values, while at the same time stopping malicious persons hijacking the beacons and repurposing them for their own requirements.

Most beacons are configured over the air using Bluetooth devices, so if they aren't properly locked down, you only need a hacker within 100 meters of your beacon to repurpose them. For example, if you place beacons all over a public place such as a mall with a weak security model, then a hacker can leave the beacons where they are and change their UIUD/major/minor triplet for their own app.

What's worse, if hackers know they can change your beacon profiles, then why not just steal them and reuse them somewhere else?

Knowing that your beacons are still where you left them is important to you as an app developer or service provider. My team at Eden Agency has deployed a number of ways to ensure that beacons are still where we designed them to be (and that they still have battery), all of which ultimately involve relying on our app consumers to walk past a beacon using our app. We then pick up the physical location using GPS and report back to a central HTTP web service.

# Dispelling security myths

We already dispelled most of the common security myths in *Chapter 1*, *Welcome to iBeacon*, but I thought I'd just reiterate them so that you've got a complete vocabulary for your wary clients or users. Consider the following steps:

- **Beacons are tracking my location**: Beacons aren't tracking your location. They're not doing anything at all except telling you they're nearby. They push data and don't receive data at all and what's more, most beacons your app comes into contact with don't even care that they are there.
- **Beacons are delivering targeted offers**: Beacons aren't delivering anything except their UUID/major/minor triplet values. In order to deliver targeted offers, your app needs to know more about your habits and so ultimately needs your permission and some other understanding about you as a person.
- **Beacons can track me without my permission**: Your mobile device will come in contact with beacons every day and as the technology gains momentum, your device will *encounter* thousands of beacons. Beacons don't pull any data from your device and in order for any app to notify the developer of your location, you need to have given permission to location information first.
- **My UUID belongs to me**: The UUID doesn't belong to you; you might generate it and it's impossible for somebody else to generate the same one by accident, but since there's no governing body looking after which UUID belongs to whom, there's nothing to stop people using the same UUID as you.

# Overcoming users' fears with good UX

As with any new technology, it's important to alleviate your users' fears about their privacy with a good UI.

Instead of just using the default location permission dialog box, it's important to tell the user why you want permission for their location with a full description. What's more, since iOS 7, you have been able to add this description using the `NSLocationUsageDescription` key in the app's `info.plist` file.

It's also important to ask for location at a relevant point; don't just spring the request on your user as soon as they start the app; otherwise, they're likely to deny your request.

Finally, only get the location if you have to. There's no quicker way to get a user to delete your app than by spamming them with marketing messages.

My final piece of advice when developing apps with beacons is to look at your app as a user and not just a developer. If your piece of functionality *feels* right from a user perspective, then it is. If you ask yourself whether a user might see your app as snooping, then the chances are that you're not providing the user with enough valuable functionality to request the user's location.

# Summary

In this chapter, we discussed some of the security issues surrounding iBeacon deployment and ways to protect against some of those security issues. Finally, we discussed common fears of users who encounter iBeacon solutions and ways to alleviate those fears.

We've come to the end of the chapter and your initial journey into iBeacon solutions, but this is by no means the end of your journey. If you have any questions at all about the book, then I'd love to hear from you, catch me on Twitter at `@craiggilchrist` and I'll gladly help you out. All that remains is to wish you the best of luck with your future proximity-powered endeavors from myself and everyone involved in the book. Thank you for reading and I hope you build incredible iBeacon solutions.

# Index

## A

**accuracy property** 68
**advert**
 displaying 49-51
**AirDrop** 7
**airline assistance**
 use case for 88
**AltBeacon** 130, 131
**anatomy**
 viewing 94
**Antwerp Museum**
 URL 11
**API access**
 adding 135
**app**
 background mode, enabling 126
 beacons, testing 105
 beginning, with database schema 113
 building 58, 113
 helper, using 114-116
 NSLocationAlwaysUsageDescription, adding 126
 passbook pass, testing 105
 responsibility, handling 89
 testing 104, 127, 145
**app delegate**
 configuring 96-98
**atrium view, iBeacon museum app**
 about 150
 configuring 165
 controls, adding 165-167

## B

**background**
 beacons, ranging 111
**background modes**
 enabling 126
 system, cheating 113
 used, for keeping location 112
**beacon**
 about 107
 distance, receiving 102
 hacking 171
 ranging 100
 ranging, in background 111
 security myths, dispelling 172
 spoofing 169
 spoofing, defending against 170, 171
 stickers 110, 111
 testing 105
 users' fears, overcoming with UX 172
 UUIDs, rotating 171
**beacon:accelerometerStateChanged: task, ESTBeaconDelegate** 133
**beacon:didDisconnectWithError: task, ESTBeaconDelegate** 132
**beaconConnectionDidFail:withError: task, ESTBeaconDelegate** 132
**beaconConnectionDidSucceeded: task, ESTBeaconDelegate** 132
**beacon manager, master view controller**
 configuring 137
**beacons, detail view controller**
 connecting 140, 141
 disconnecting 140, 141
**beacons, iBeacon museum app**
 ranging 163, 164
**beacons, master view controller**
 ranging 121
**Belkin WeMo**
 about 109

URL 109
**Bluetooth Low Energy (BLE)** 7, 56
**broadcast values**
   obtaining, from CLBeaconRegion 57

## C

**CBCentral class** 56
**CBPeripheral class** 57
**CBPeripheralManager class** 57
**centrals** 56
**CLBeaconRegion**
   about 36
   broadcast values, obtaining from 57
**CLBeaconRegion, options**
   CLBeaconRegion.notifyEntryState
      OnDisplay 90
   CLBeaconRegion.notifyOnEntry 90
   CLBeaconRegion.notifyOnExit 90
**CLLocationManager class**
   about 37
   defining, line by line 37, 38
   locationManager:didChangeAuthorization
      Status 40
   locationManager:didEnterRegion 38
   locationManager:didExitRegion 39
   locationManager:didRangeBeacons:
      inRegion 39
**CLLocationManagerDelegate method**
   configuring 27
   writing up 47, 48
**CLLocationManager instance**
   adding 28
**CLOfferViewController**
   adding 43
**CLProximity enum values**
   CLProximityFar 69
   CLProximityImmediate 69
   CLProximityNear 69
   CLProximityUnknown 69
**commercial applications, iBeacon** 11
**companion app**
   URL 21
   using 22, 23
**companion OS X application** 21, 22
**compatible devices, iBeacon** 10
**Consumer Electronics Show (CES)** 169

**content methods, iBeacon museum app**
   adding 162
**controls**
   adding 44, 45
   setting up 59
**controls, iBeacon museum app**
   adding 158-160
   adding, to exhibit view 161
**Core Bluetooth framework**
   about 7, 55, 56
   CBCentral class 56
   CBPeripheral class 57
   CBPeripheralManager class 57
**Core Data framework, master
    view controller**
   data, fetching from 118
   URL 118
**Core Location framework**
   about 7, 36
   adding 26
   CLBeaconRegion class 36
   CLLocationManager class 37
**CoreLocation functionality, iBeacon
    museum app**
   adding 155

## D

**database schema**
   app, beginning with 113
**detail view controller**
   beacons, connecting 140, 141
   beacons, disconnecting 140, 141
   changes, saving 141-143
   configuring 138
   implementing 122
   input, validating 125
   properties, obtaining 124
   properties, setting 124
   UI, finishing off 125, 126
   view, configuring 123, 139
**down badges**
   clearing 100

## E

**ESTBeacon** 132

ESTBeaconDelegate
    about 132
    beacon:accelerometerStateChanged:
        task 133
    beacon:didDisconnectWithError: task 132
    beaconConnectionDidFail:withError:
        task 132
    beaconConnectionDidSucceeded: task 132
ESTBeaconManager 133
ESTBeaconManagerDelegate 133
Estimote
    about 13
    and SDK 129
    development tutorials 14
    tools 14
    URL 131
Estimote API 2.1
    security 131
    using 131
Estimote API pages
    URL 131
Estimote beacons
    cons 15
    pros 15
Estimote SDK classes
    about 132
    adding 134
    ESTBeacon 132
    ESTBeaconDelegate 132
    ESTBeaconManager 133
    ESTBeaconManagerDelegate 133
exhibitions, iBeacon museum app 148
exhibit view, iBeacon museum app
    about 150
    configuring 160, 161
    controls, adding 161

# F

frameworks
    adding 59

# G

gender
    selecting 103, 104
Geo-fencing (geofencing) 36
global positioning system (GPS) 36

# H

hacking, Beacon 171
Hello world
    about 23, 24
    CLLocationManagerDelegate method,
        configuring 27, 28
    CLLocationManager instance, adding 28
    code, breaking 29
    code, testing 30-32
    Core Location framework, adding 25
    monitoring, starting 28
    permission message, adding 27
    UUID, preparing 28
helper class
    about 135, 136
    using 114-116
home automation
    about 107
    and iBeacon 109, 110
hunter view controller, treasure hunting app
    building 78
    code, completing 85
    imports 80
    private properties 80
    public properties 80
    region, entering 82
    region, exiting 82
    state, changing 82-84
    states 79, 80
    tidying up 85
    view, loading 81

# I

iBeacon
    about 7
    and home automation 109, 110
    commercial applications 11, 12
    compatible iOS devices 10
    permissions 40, 41
    security 169
iBeacon museum app
    about 149
    building 153
    design 152
    exhibitions 147, 148
    iBeacon university, URL 150

[ 177 ]

structure 149
supporting website 150
testing 167
user's journey, tracking 151, 152
**iBeacon museum app, building**
atrium view, configuring 165
atrium view controls, adding 165-167
beacons, ranging 163, 164
content methods, adding 162
controls, adding 158-160
controls, adding to exhibit view 161, 162
CoreLocation functionality, adding 155
exhibit view, configuring 160, 161
first view, determining 155, 156
permission view, configuring 157, 158
project, creating 153
views, initializing 153, 154
**iBeacon museum app, views**
atrium view 150
exhibit view 150
permission view 149
**iBeacon university**
URL 148
**images, treasure hunting app**
adding 73, 74
**imports, hunter view controller 80**
**input, detail view controller**
validating 125

## L

**location manager**
configuring 46, 47
**locationManager:didChangeAuthorization**
**Status 40**
**locationManager:didEnterRegion 38**
**locationManager:didExitRegion 39**
**locationManager:didRangeBeacons:**
**inRegion 39**
**location permission, settings**
advert, displaying 49-51
CLLocationManagerDelegate,
writing up 47, 48
controls, adding 44, 45
location manager, configuring 46, 47
offer, dismissing 51-53
root view controller, setting up 45

**locations**
enabling, after denial 42
keeping, background modes used 112
NSLocationAlwaysUsageDescription 42
NSLocationWhenInUseUsage
Description 42
permissions, in iOS 8 41

## M

**Macy's**
URL 11
**Made for iPhone (MFi) 7**
**Major League Baseball**
URL 11
**major value, UUID 35**
**Make hack**
URL 169
**master view controller**
about 133
beacons, ranging 121
configuring 136
data, fetching from Core Data
framework 118
implementing 116
new objects, inserting 121
table cell, configuring 119, 120
user, notifying 120
view controller, configuring 117
**measured power 9**
**minor value, UUID 35**
**N**
**Near Field Communication (NFC) 7**
**Nest**
about 108
URL 108
**Ninja Blocks**
about 108
URL 107, 108
**NSLocationAlwaysUsageDescription**
about 42
adding 126
**NSLocationWhenInUse**
**UsageDescription 42**

## O

objects, master view controller
    inserting 121

## P

passbook
    integration 91-93
passbook pass
    adding 104
    testing 105
peripherals 55
permission message
    adding 27
permissions, iBeacon
    about 40
    location, in iOS 8 41
permission view, iBeacon museum app
    about 149
    configuring 157, 158
Phillips Hue
    about 109
    URL 109
platform
    selecting 130
project, iBeacon museum app
    creating 153
properties, detail view controller
    getting 124
    setting 124
protocol data unit (PDU) 131
proximity property 68
public properties, hunter view controller 80

## R

radio frequency identification (RFID) 36
range 9
Raspberry Pi
    about 108
    URL 107, 108
received strength signal indication (RSSI) 9
RedBear Beacon B1
    cons 20
    pros 19
RedBear BeaconTool app
    URL 18

RedBearLab
    cons 18, 19
regions
    entering 99, 100
    exiting 99, 100
retail loyalty
    use case for 88
root view controller
    setting up 45
root view controller, treasure hunting app
    building 74, 75
ROXIMITY
    about 15-17
    implementing 130
ROXIMITY Beacon Explorer app
    URL 17
ROXIMITY beacons
    cons 17
    pros 17

## S

SDK
    and Estimote 129
security, Beacon
    myths, dispelling 172
security, Estimote API 2.1 131
states, hunter view controller
    about 79, 80
    changing 82-84
storyboard
    wiring up 61
switch logic
    adding 63-65

## T

table cell, master view controller
    configuring 119, 120
treasure hunting app
    about 67-71
    building 71
    distance 68
    frameworks, adding 73
    hunter view controller, building 78
    images, adding 73, 74
    initial views, drawing 72
    project settings, adding 73

root view controller, building 74, 75
treasure view controller, building 75-78
wiring up 78
**treasure view controller, treasure hunting app**
building 75-78
**tutorial app**
about 93, 111
advert, showing 49-51
anatomy, viewing 94
app delegate, configuring 96-98
application, creating 95
beacons, ranging 100
building 43
CLLocationManagerDelegate, wiring up 47, 48
CLOfferViewController, adding 43, 44
code 95
controls, adding 44, 45
creating 43
down badges, clearing 100
location manager, configuring 46, 47
location permission, setting 44
no ranging, in background 98
offer, dismissing 51-53
regions, entering 99
regions, exiting 99
root view controller, setting up 45, 46
scenario 93, 94
view controller, implementing 101
view, creating 95, 96
**TXPower** 58

# U

**UI, detail view controller**
finishing off 125, 126
**Universally Unique Identifier.** *See* **UUID**
**use case**
for airline assistance 88
for retail loyalty 88
**use case, UUID** 35
**user, master view controller**
notifying 120
**users' fears**
overcoming, with UX 172

**user's journey, iBeacon museum app**
tracking 151, 152
**UUID**
about 8, 9, 33-35
major value 8, 35
minor value 8, 35
preparing 28
rotating 171
use case, example 35

# V

**vendor**
about 12, 13
options 20
**view**
creating 60, 95, 96
**view controller**
beacon distance, receiving 102
gender, selecting 103, 104
passbook pass, adding 104, 105
setting up 62, 63
view, initializing 101, 102
**view, detail view controller**
configuring 123, 139
creating 144
**view, hunter view controller**
loading 81
**views, iBeacon museum app**
first view, determining 155, 156
initializing 153, 154
**Virgin Atlantic**
URL 11

# W

**Waze app**
URL 90
**website, iBeacon museum app**
supporting 150
**World Wide Web (WWW)** 108

# X

**Xcode**
implementing 133

# [PACKT PUBLISHING] Thank you for buying Learning iBeacon

## About Packt Publishing

Packt, pronounced 'packed', published its first book "*Mastering phpMyAdmin for Effective MySQL Management*" in April 2004 and subsequently continued to specialize in publishing highly focused books on specific technologies and solutions.

Our books and publications share the experiences of your fellow IT professionals in adapting and customizing today's systems, applications, and frameworks. Our solution based books give you the knowledge and power to customize the software and technologies you're using to get the job done. Packt books are more specific and less general than the IT books you have seen in the past. Our unique business model allows us to bring you more focused information, giving you more of what you need to know, and less of what you don't.

Packt is a modern, yet unique publishing company, which focuses on producing quality, cutting-edge books for communities of developers, administrators, and newbies alike. For more information, please visit our website: www.packtpub.com.

## Writing for Packt

We welcome all inquiries from people who are interested in authoring. Book proposals should be sent to author@packtpub.com. If your book idea is still at an early stage and you would like to discuss it first before writing a formal book proposal, contact us; one of our commissioning editors will get in touch with you.

We're not just looking for published authors; if you have strong technical skills but no writing experience, our experienced editors can help you develop a writing career, or simply get some additional reward for your expertise.

# [PACKT] PUBLISHING

## Near Field Communication with Android Cookbook

ISBN: 978-1-78328-965-3　　　Paperback: 286 pages

Discover the endless possibilities of using Android NFC capabilities to enhance your apps over 50 practical recipes

1. Practical and real-life examples showing how and where NFC can be used.
2. Discover how to exploit NFC capabilities to enhance your apps to easily share and interact with the world.
3. Learn how to extend cross-device content sharing by taking advantage of Android Beam's capabilities.

## iOS and OS X Network Programming Cookbook

ISBN: 978-1-84969-808-5　　　Paperback: 300 pages

Over 50 recipes to develop network applications in both the iOS and OS X environment

1. Use several Apple and third-party APIs to develop both server and client networked applications.
2. Shows you how to integrate all of the third-party libraries and APIs with your applications.
3. Includes sample projects for both iOS and OS X environments.

Please check **www.PacktPub.com** for information on our titles

## Arduino Home Automation Projects

ISBN: 978-1-78398-606-4     Paperback: 132 pages

Automate your home using the powerful Arduino platform

1. Interface home automation components with Arduino.
2. Automate your projects to communicate wirelessly using XBee, Bluetooth, and Wi-Fi.
3. Build seven exciting, instruction-based home automation projects with Arduino in no time.

## Application Development in iOS 7

ISBN: 978-1-78355-031-9     Paperback: 126 pages

Learn how to build an entire real-world application using all of iOS 7's new features

1. Get acquainted with the new features of iOS 7 through real-world, project-based learning.
2. Take an in-depth look at Xcode 5, Foundation, and autolayout.
3. Utilize the full source code and assets present to build an actual interactive application.

Please check **www.PacktPub.com** for information on our titles

Printed in Great Britain
by Amazon.co.uk, Ltd.,
Marston Gate.